To Da...

~ *r*~/ :

Books by Gerry Marcotte

An Eclectic Gathering

I'm Here But Not All There

Gerry Marcotte

T. G. I. F.

TOLERANCE

GRATITUDE

INTEGRITY

FORGIVENESS

Chronicler Publishing

For information address:
Chronicler Publishing
104 Jones Beach,
RR 1 Evansburg,
Alberta, Canada, T0E 0T0
www.chroniclerpublishing.com

ISBN: 9780980953473

Dedications

To Aunt Lucille...My guiding light...Through your strength and determination, you have shown me what fortitude means...plus the wisdom and insight that you have passed on to me is immeasurable...You are my anchor, my symbol of hope...and I thank you kindly for that...I love you so very much.

To Kathy...I have chosen a path that includes you...and because of this choice, I am headed in the right direction...today...I am very grateful to have you as the love of my life...

Acknowledgments

These are the people who have made this book possible:

* To my editor and publisher, Charles O Goulet. Always a smile, always a word of encouragement…and, at times a little nudge. You have continuously made me feel that my works, my poems were not written in vain…and for that I thank-you.

* A special thanks to Denise Goulet for the encouragement she has given me. I want to thank both her and Charlie for the many hours we spent in discussing the many different topics we felt needed our help…or at least our comments. I don't ever recall solving even one of these 'so called' important issues. I guess the only wisdom that was called for was the observations you made on some of my poems.

* To my personal friends…and you all know who you are. Many of the poems are a reflection of your teachings to me…teachings of tolerance, gratitude, integrity and forgiveness…and I thank you for your honesty.

* To Al Hagman…Thanks for letting me publish your beautiful poem…It truly touches my heart.

* To my family…Thanks for your love.

* To all the varied people in the poems…Thank-you for your stories, and for giving me the opportunity to project these stories through my pen…

* Cover by Jamie Blahun, thanks, much appreciated.

Gratitude

T.G.I.F. (Tolerance, Gratitude, Integrity, Forgiveness) is my third book of poems. If you read any or all of my previous two books, you will see that this book certainly has a different feel concerning the poems I've written. My writings are a reflection of where I'm at on my journey called Life. I can honestly say that it's been quite a ride…I've met a lot of interesting, engaging people, and thankfully a few have remained close friends.

I want to thank all who have taken a chance on my type of writing. I know it's a different style, in spite of the fact that most of the poems are based on life issues. I also know that, for the most part, all of us have had similar experiences as those expressed by me in these poems. I like to call my poems "Stories in Verse", for that is really what they are. Unfortunately, many people have not, and I suspect will not read my works because, they tell me, they don't like poetry…At least they're honest, and I want to thank them for that.

To all…Feel free to give me feedback on this book, or my previous books, *An Eclectic Gathering,* and *I'm Here But Not All There*…and I thank you in advance.

My e-mail is mailto:jagm@xplornet.com

Gerry Marcotte

Praise For

TGIF Tolerance Gratitude Integrity Forgiveness

He's done it again! Brought to life in poetic form what so many of us feel and think but can't quite find the words to express. *TGIF-Tolerance, Gratitude, Integrity, Forgiveness.* Who hasn't been able to relate to those words? Leave it to Gerry Marcotte to put a whimsical spin on the human frailties we all encounter as we come face to face with ourselves. Once again Gerry crafts his thoughts and feelings into words that hold nothing back; tackling often delicate and uncomfortable subjects. Whether you align with his perception and life experiences or not, Gerry's writing challenges the reader to dig deeper to a place of personal honesty and openness while being entertained by his unique poet expression.

I have immense respect for Gerry as a person, a friend and an accomplished and incredibly talented author. I trust all who read Gerry Marcotte's work will find that their time has been well spent!

Jamie Blahun... Founder of ***Women at the Well.***

I'm Here But Not All There.

For me, reading poetry, like listening to music, is a most personal kind of experience. The writer must strike a balance between truthfully capturing his thoughts and feelings, and uniquely creating a work that is accessible and interesting for either the reader or listener.

Gerry Marcotte is most successful in finding that balance. In his book *I'm Here But Not All There*, his poems are intensely personal yet universal in theme. His subject matter, while varied, never strays too far from his own experience, and Gerry typically attacks common struggle and experience with style and originality. His is a unique writing voice that grows bolder with each collection.

Jory Nash...Singer/Songwriter...*new blue day*

Table Of Contents

T. G. I. F.
(Tolerance, Gratitude, Integrity, Forgiveness)

To live and let live…What does that mean? Acceptance…
being accommodating to both similarity and difference…
Concerning individual beliefs…tolerance lets you select
what you feel comfortable with…and not judge others
viewpoints, shortcomings, and opinions…Things that matter…
To understand Tolerance is to understand respect…

A feeling is a fleeting emotion, usually passing quickly by…
yet, frequently Gratitude is mistaken for this sentiment…
Gratitude is a gift…something freely given…an excitement…
something to be remembered, which often makes us cry
tears of joy…This gift may be a lesson in meekness …
or merely a thank-you. Whatever…it leaves nothing to guess…

Honesty, truth, veracity…the yardstick in measuring
the core values of a person…This is, in essence, Integrity…
In effect, it takes someone who is determined, who is gritty…
not afraid to step to the plate for what he believes…yet, ensuring
his modesty, his gentleness…Integrity truly begins with oneself…
There's nothing better than a clear conscience…That's true wealth…

At times in life we end up with a deep emotional hurt…
something we will never forget…Anger and resentment
set in…feelings we can't let in…If we let them rent
space in our minds, we lose…Therefore, we must insert
Forgiveness…We must let go…Our Creator will abet…
if asked…Forgiveness leads to be forgiven…A sure bet…

I Guess God Had Other Plans For You.

On March 03, 2005, four RCMP Constables were murdered while investigating a marijuana grow operation and stolen vehicle/parts on the farm of Jim Roszko, situated at Rochfort Bridge...not far from Mayerthorpe. The murderer, Jim Roszko, after being shot and wounded, committed suicide. The four Mounties were Constables Peter Schiemann, Leo Johnston, Anthony Gordon and Brock Myrol.

This poem is written from my feelings of this devastating event. In this poem I tried to imagine how the wives/ fiancée of these four officers felt. I know I could never experience that feeling, especially with the way they died, yet I have experienced the loss of a loved one through cancer. To finally find peace of mind I had to go through the grieving process...denial, fear, anger, hate...until finally I achieved acceptance... acceptance that they were gone. As time passes, the pain of their loss is less, yet I never forget them...in fact there are few day I don't think of them.

I know that not all had children, nor even all were married...but each had a loved one, be it spouse, fiancée, and, of course, family.

I know that this poem is merely one in hundreds of documents, letters, reports, poems written by many different people, concerning these tragic deaths. To some this poem may mean nothing or very little...for their documents are far more important...at least to them...but that's not why I wrote this poem...no...I wrote it so I could express feelings of empathy for those left behind.

When I try to figure out what the end results of this sad incident are going to be, I'm at a loss like most...but there is always good that comes out of tragedy. Why God chose these people and this type of incident...only He knows...What He has planned, again only He knows...but I truly feel His plans for these four men...and their families...will work out for all...but, only in His time. Until then, unfortunately much hurt and pain will continue to be felt.

I make no judgment on Jim Roszko...I'll let God do that.

I Guess God Had Other Plans For You.

When I heard the news…I wanted to die…
How could that be…You promised me you'd be back.
We kissed this morning, then you whispered in my ear…
those few precious words…"I love you so much…"
Now you're deceased!
Oh God! You must have made a mistake…tell me so.
Let me hear his voice…see his smile…touch his face…
Please help me…I'm so lost…I don't know what to do…

When I awoke, I wasn't sure if I had been dreaming,
or if my feelings were really telling me the truth…
though I gotta say I didn't sleep all that well.
They tell me you're really gone…to be strong…
I don't believe them…
You always liked to play little jokes…I'm sure this is one…
Oh honey! Please come home…I love you so much…
I know all was not perfect, but good things were happening.

Remember the first time you told me you loved me?
I certainly do…I was ecstatic…My dream was coming true…
No words could have been better spoken. Oh! I loved you.
I dreamt of completeness: True friends/cherished lovers.
No More! Total Silence…
Oh God, help me…I hate that terrible man so, so much…
In one fell swoop, he completely shattered all our dreams
If there is a place worse than hell…make sure he goes there.

My tears keep flowing and flowing…My heart aches so much,
with such poignant pain…imagining your last moments…your last thoughts.
I visualize you so brave…doing what you truly loved…To Protect…
I tried to imagine your feelings…when you realized you were dying…
And do you know what? I could never imagine how you felt…
though I tried…In my mind's eye, what I conceived paled to reality…
yet a chill seized my body… I have never experienced such coldness…
such a feeling of total loss, total despondency. Death is so final!

3

The kids miss you tremendously...as do I. They don't understand...nor do I.
You truly loved them...and me...Why did your sunset come so early?
Folks have been truly helpful...and I appreciate it...but I wish it wasn't so...
You have left a void...leaving me with a hurt unexplainable empty feeling.
We are now going down a road never before traveled...and it's scary...
They tell me life goes on...Perhaps...but, today I'm not so sure that's true.
Come home, sweetheart...things are falling apart...We need you so much...
We need your wisdom, your knowledge, your strength and fortitude...

So few of us will do anything of significance that will have an impact
on society. Most will be remembered merely by a handful of people.
You, on the other hand, will be remembered by many...unfortunately...
Circumstances are trying to make you into someone you weren't...
You never looked for the limelight...you were too in-tuned with self...
yet, you have been portrayed as a hero...I know, you would just shudder.
To me...you were the absolute greatest...To others you were many things...
Honest, loyal, decent, fair...an okay type of guy...Is that a hero?

I'm not sure what to believe when it comes to religion and spirituality,
for, it never was important as a child...nor as an adult. I never questioned...
All of a sudden it becomes very significant...I'm really searching...
Thinking about it...Why would we have choices if we lived on instinct?
Why have morals and ethics? We don't need ideals nor a conscience,
if there is nothing when we die? I love you...I believe you're watching.
I still cry so much, not understanding. Each night I ask this Higher Power
to explain why this happened...to help us. They say He works thru people.
If that's true, then explain why He chose a killer to alter our lives completely
If God had other plans for you, he could have chosen a different route...

Good-bye sweetheart...I'll never forget...forget
how much I love you, how much I miss you, how much I long for you.
I'll never forget how fortunate I was to have had you in my life...our life...
Thank-you for your beautiful smile, your forgiving ways...your total love...
I have much to cherish of our love, so many fond memories, and the children
I wish I could take their pains, worry and fears, but I can't...We cry a lot...
Fortunately they give me the will to continue living without you, my darling.
I could never say these words enough to you: I Love You So!

4

The Guest Of Honour

Gordon Myrol was a friend. I didn't know him that long, yet I liked his style, his way of doing things. Gordon did not only talk the talk, he walked the walk...and that certainly caught my eye.

Gordon loved Jean so much. The look in his eyes told the whole story. Jean, on her part, had the same look. Such a beautiful couple. I admire them for that. Also, Gordon loved his children with a passion. He was so proud of them. The one I know is Joanne, and I felt his pride when she was around, when she was performing. He was her biggest fan. I might add...Joanne, actually is a very good musician...great voice, great style, great songwriter ...and Gordon knew that, saw that, and truly encouraged her in her pursuit.

Gordon genuinely loved his grandchildren. They were a part of him...They made him so proud. Actually they fulfilled his understanding of life, for they are his continuation. Also, Gordon loved music...that was his form of expression. He loved playing and singing...He loved life...

Thank-you Gordon for being a fine example. I think of you often. Being present at your funeral service, feeling your presence as The Guest of Honour, hearing all the kind words, the wonderful video...I was touched. Yet, through it all, I wondered if you felt comfortable with all this kindness. My personal feelings? "Hey, A Jamboree would have been more to his taste." It sure was nice knowing you. Pass on a good word!

Gordon died July 2005. The funeral certainly was a tribute to my friend. This poem is written...one verse his funeral service, the second verse my perception of his thoughts...

The Guest Of Honour

There he was…centre stage…paying attention…
really listening. Quite a crowd…some tension…
that was to be expected…but, no aggression.
That was something Gordon would not have sanctioned.

It's wonderful how we still love people…in spite of
what they are…not because of what they are…
above all family. Amazing how resilient love
truly is. This is the 'stuff' needed for guitars
and ballads…together they blend so perfectly,
conceiving words and music so idyllically.

Jean quietly took a seat close to her star.
She wanted to be near her man…not too far…
In front of him, on a stand, was his guitar…
His motto: "Music defines me…and you…who we are."

When you're hurtin' my darling, look to me
for comfort…Integrity has been the key
to our success. Our love hasn't been for free…
Because of conditions we had both agreed,
we'll keep our love alive through commitments…
that promise we made years ago…and meant.

Jamie Blahun, a good friend, who loves the blues,
sang *The Mighty Peace*, a song written and produced
by Joanne…for her dad. Trying to understand…to construe
her despondency, her sadness…solace was her clue.

Have we learnt from our mistakes, our past?
One thing...the past is what it's really all about...
Today would not be if the mould hadn't been cast
yesterday. All the joys, sorrows, certainty and doubts...
our experiences gained by self or together,
would not be...and these are...forever and ever...

Gordon is quite biased when it comes to Joanne...
She loves her dad and his brand of music.
Today, circumstances has it that he's her biggest fan...
What he dreamt of, she's attained...by taking the licks.

 I sure got rid of a lot of baggage
 over the years. It seemed to happen in stages.
 Some, which I'd accumulated, was outrageous...
 yet, some I still carry throughout our ages.
 Life is a big challenge...every single day...
 Having had you by my side, my thanks I pray.

David, Jean and Gordon's son, eulogized his father.
I sensed Gordon was smiling at all this praise...
even if, for him, it wasn't something he sought after...
No!... for others maybe...though he loves his son...his ways.

 The wake of my life is merely a path left behind...
 Ah! But what a story this trail may well tell...
 The dots between birth and death...and they're mine.
 In longevity...some to discard, some to corral.
 In retrospect, I appreciate I wasn't simply a person
 capable of loving...No, I was a loving person.

The Master of Ceremonies, Rick, introduced Dwayne...
a man of the Good Book...and a friend of Gordon's.
He talked of many things...compassion and pain,
honesty and trust... attributes Gordon did not shun.

Isn't life a bag of tricks? Thinking I've gained,
I end up further back. A bit of humility?
Life is not weakness and fault...laying blame...
No! Life's about strength and virtues...ability
to look at and appreciate the whole.
Protecting the mind and body, protects the soul.

Music and Myrols...similar to peas in a pod...
they just go so well together...A tradition.
Most members sing and play whatever's sought...
by taking turns. Sometimes it's more fun to listen.

Gordon taught his children...and his siblings
that it wasn't so important to be the best...
No! It was way more significant to bring
a good attitude, and to honestly do your best.
Happiness and success are things you bestow
to the world...In return you gain serenity and repose.

Well, his family sang and played a few numbers...
This was Gordon's type of music. I could envision
him outdoors, strumming away in the heat of summer,
family all around, big smile, loving the situation.

So few of us will be truly appreciated...
even though in time we tried to persuade, to cajole,
to no avail. In fact, the wise know their fate...
for them it just means playing the same role.
Reviewing ones life...most of us are not capable
to give very much...yet, we offer what we're able.

To be The Guest of Honour is a special privilege...
Something to be cherished, something to be treasured.
This is where family and friends acknowledged
his attributes, his traits, which were many... Let's listen to him...

"Let me give you a few of my feelings:
Watch your thoughts, for words will follow.
Where there are words, there is also action.
Realize this, for they become habits...nothing shallow.
Study these before they cause too many reactions,
or become part of your life-style, your character...
This is your moral fibre...your calling card...
which leads to your fate...past, present and future...
If played properly, there are many great rewards."

"I've led a good life, I've led a simple life...
my benefits were many...A loving, beautiful wife,
devoted children whom caused me very little strife,
and grand kids I just adored while I was alive.
What more could I have ask for? Thank-you. God Bless."

Life, The Banquet.

A while back, I wrote a poem, and in my introduction I talked of the banquet of life, and how many had left this table starving. Over the years this phrase stayed with me, helping me be more aware of my choices and actions. I feel I've gained by it, for I feel I've become less judgmental, less negative thinking, more patience... thought I still don't have a lot...more assertiveness, and many may laugh at that. For the most part, I have become a better person...I think!

As I also mentioned in the other poem, I feel there is something after death. Of course, I'll only find out when I die if this true or not...In the mean time it's immaterial if there or isn't...I have the right and the choice to follow the course I ought...as each of us has this choice...and this is the course I choose. I'm certainly not here to judge what others think and feel. We are all individuals...therefore we all have our own thoughts on this subject...

I wrote this poem based on a smorgasbord...a mixture of thoughts, feelings, morals, viewpoints...my attitude... and how they controlled my life and what may be the end results for me because of this attitude. All I can say is that it's interesting what I came up with... just a little deeper level in trying to figure out me. Will this banquet happen or be worth it all? I have no answer...but what have I got to lose?

Life, The Banquet.

How I was selected to live on this earth...
why my cell was chosen...No one can answer.
Where I was born...be it by a fireside, a hearth,
or fancy hospital matters not...life did occur.
I am here! Now the banquet has commenced...
My choices taken from now and this time hence
will determine the life I'll lead and also whence.

Life is truly a labyrinth...much complexity...a maze...
The closer I come to understanding it's ways,
the more I realize that I have merely grazed
on what it entails...Yet, when I think of death,
I've come to understand that my last breathe
is merely my physical end...my corporal rest...
Now the true test results...choices I've made
to better my life will determine my accolades.

Wow! Are these banquet rooms ever large...massive...
In the physical mind...it encompasses the whole planet...
In the emotional mind...many rooms are attractive,
and in the spiritual mind...well...the Creator is it ...
which includes the whole universe... Inconceivable!
Being born has made this banquet very feasible.
Life's issues determine the different tables I will visit.
Many I will only look at, but at some I will sit.

Utterly amazing...A room, of which I cannot see the end...
and this room is designated strictly to EGO...
I've felt many of these dishes...None I wish to defend.
I guess, over time, I certainly have mellowed...
All these servings have a self-importance attachment...
ego-centric, ego-mania, ego-ist, ego-involvement.
I can't do it on my own...though I certainly did try...
Finally, I had to change directions...I had to say good-bye.

11

To be privileged, to have choices,
I must foremost settle my demons...
By listening to my inner voices,
my beliefs, I'll experience the sun,
instead of feeling just not right.
What does that mean? Insight!
I don't have to live in fright...

Who all comes to this feast? Is everybody invited?
The program must be gargantuan. Who would write it?
The amount of souls here seem to be divided.
A small number are really enjoying the festivities...
They're into all the really neat and nifty goodies,
and seem not to worry. They've found the right keys...
or better yet, they've followed their conscience.
Their ethics, morals and principles have no pretense.

Would you believe that! A gigantic room loaded with fear.
Big dishes of worry, concern, anxiety, apprehension,
and bigger dishes of fright...Like looking in a mirror...
In my wary vision I also see dread and trepidation.
I look across the way and lo and behold I see sanguine...
These are the tables I want to be a part of...to dine...
Table upon table of cheerfulness, hope and courage.
I'll be able to partake if I'm sage, not full of rage.

Isn't that neat? I've recognized some of the souls...
and a few don't seem to be enjoying this feast.
I perceive that they feel like they're on parole...
Maybe I'm wrong, but I sense little peace.
Ah, but some of the others that I identified
were laughing and joking, obviously satisfied.
Most carried plates over-flowing with love...
I sure hope that is something I'll get enough of.

Don't quit living before your time comes...
life's too short. At times, take some chances...
Mistakes are where you learn your options,
so...some risks will truly enhance,
really improve your quality of life...
Be honest with self...really strive.
When this happens, you'll have arrived.

Life is a smorgasbord: A numerous array
of circumstance and situations...on display...
in many forms, styles, and indeed in many ways.
This elaborate feast has so, so much to offer...
Love, peace, joy, happiness are used to lure,
but, nearby are hate, war, resentments and anger.
My choices...Do I want to enjoy this feast,
or do I share my misery with the beast.

No one asked me if I wanted to be born...not my choice...
but, today, I really can't see myself not being here.
I've lived long enough to have, at times, some poise...
for, I've been taught to really listen...to use my ears...
instead of pretending I know many things. Even if I dawdle,
while the hour-glass sand sifts slowly through the vessel,
death'll still happen. This process, which originated at birth,
will be facilitated by my choices...They'll decide my worth.

In reviewing my life...my family, my children, my health,
my friends, and for sure my passions...These are my mainstay...
these are my support, my foundation...This is my wealth...
Even if I lost my job, house, or car...I'd still be okay.
Also, if I understand not to put too much emphasis
on trifle issues...for many are impulsive...so impetuous,
then my priorities will include big doses of happiness
and contentment...If so, my chances'll be good at the fest.

I Won't Give Up.

My very personal friend is not having a good time lately. I know of some of the issues at play, and I can correctly guess at some of the other issues, but there are some I can suspect...but that's it. She will have to evaluate them, test them, perhaps discuss them...but the end result is her decision, and sometimes that is a tough thing to make.

She is such a good person...So loving...so compassionate, so caring, and so forgiving. All excellent qualities...Unfortunately some take advantage of her kindness.

I admire her strong will, her strong belief in a Creator. At one time her reputation may have been one of disdain because of her life-style. Today I can assure you her reputation is exemplary...a model of self-respect... a proud/humble person.

You have helped me to understand me. You're a true friend...not afraid to stick-up for me if people want to slander me, yet not afraid to suggest when you feel I'm not right. Thank-you, my friend. Now it's my turn to help you look at some challenging issues, issues that have been very persistent and draining...This, of course, is from my perspective...my point of view. I know you won't quit, you won't give up even though, at times, it would be a lot easier. Live for today, my friend. Good things will happen... just like the promises guarantee.

Love you lots.

I Won't Give Up...

Life is a contradiction...a hassle really.
Expectations contravene logic most times...
and truly, thinking about it, it's so silly.
Actually the weight is becoming cumbersome.
In the near distance, I softly hear the chimes...
telling me to take a varied path...to help my mind,
body and soul...They're tired from this climb.

What I am will never change I'm quite sure...
but who I am is always changing. For this to concur,
depends on how I want to play the hand I was dealt.
If nothing else, I have to take care of myself...
first...Lately I tend to put me close to last...
Similar to what I use to do in my past.

I try and analyze what I feel...my values...
to understand what's important, what's true...
at least to me...What I see is a frozen river,
and stillness my disguise...That gives me a shiver...
for I know the current is still there though hidden...
like my feelings. My mind's struggling...truly striven.

To take a different path is to ask myself...
"Do I want this life? Will it improve my health?"
I need to listen to my soul for answers,
and silence is the key for this to occur,
for me to fathom, to probe my sense of direction,
in understanding the different segments, different factions.

Perhaps I need to distinguish between the life
that I'm leading...the one with so much strife...
and the life I dream about...love, compassion,
empathy and kindness...and, of course, lots of fun...
Actually, I'd be happy with some appreciation,
some respect...That would instigate exhilaration.

I won't go back to my former life...no way...
yet, many issues haven't changed even though I pray.
But in saying that, really, so much has transformed,
yet, why do I still feel nothing's the norm?
I know to better myself I made my amends...
So why is the load I carry making me bend?

Much of the baggage I still carry is called love...
love of my children, my family...Important stuff...
My Creator made this possible...They're on my watch.
I can't give up on them...I've invested too much...
But...this role has, unfortunately, taken it's toll.
My spirits are weary...I also need to be consoled.

Other side of coin...Some are intent to waylay
me...Through their tactics, there is no desire to parley...
Because of their dirty, sneaky actions, I feel crushed.
I perceive I've been tarred by a stroke of a brush...
From a distance...it's so easy to criticize, to condemn...
I'm the lucky one...I can forgive...That is my gem.
But to be honest...today...I won't exonerate them.

Something today that I would never trade...
is my fortitude to ask my Creator for aid,
for help...It certainly helps with the stress.
Perhaps what He sees is one heck of a mess...
and not totally sure how to rearrange...
or maybe He feels it's time for me to change.

There's a dawn to every night...Something to remember,
especially when I inadvertently forget to consider
my feelings, believing I know all, asking no one for consent.
For me to be at peace, I have to live in the present...
plus, I need to be in tune with my surroundings and me.
Dawn will then arrive...shedding some light...letting me see.

In reviewing my past, I come to understand,
and realize why I had to leave my home, my band...
My life today is the result...I did regret...but no more...
Most days I love me...where it use to be quite a chore...
Today, I have only today...tomorrow never comes...
so, I live this day to it's fullest...no regrets, no qualms...

I won't give up...no possible way! I have too much
to live for...What I need is get back my touch...
What it entails is to take a step back...an inventory.
I'll need willingness and honesty for a valid story...
Then right choices can be made...with less worry.

17

I Leave You With A Thought.

Everyone has heard the statement: " I don't want my kids to go through the hardships I went through…" What does that mean to you? For myself, what I think it means is, "I want my kids to have more material wealth than I had as a kid." That really sounds so compassionate, so caring, but honestly thinking about it…is it such a good thing?

In today's society, we measure success with money. If you have a big new house with beautiful furniture, a new or newer car or SUV…or both, making big wages, can afford all the new toys on the market…holiday trailer, dirt bike, boat, cabin at the lake, etc…have a computer for each member of the family, the latest in IPODS…and the list goes on…then, in the eyes of many, you are rich and a true success…and as long as material gains keep happening, things will be great, and ego will run the show.

What happens when you get sick, or unfortunately lose your job…for whatever reason, or the market drops? Hopefully you have pensions or reserves of sorts, but after all is said and done, you may have to downsize, reduce the toys, find a less paying job. All of a sudden security may become an issue, plus the accolades of your equal are no longer. In following my argument, this would mean you are no longer a success… at least according to your peers.

I remember a time, not so very long ago, where our family went and visited other families for entertainment…We went as a family to a drive-in, or a movie, or to the lake for a picnic. We rarely went out to eat, plus we always ate our meals as a family unit. Today, a family outing is "The Mall." A family meal is at McDonalds… Businesses are open 7 days a week, and so many parents and children have to work to maintain the life-style they have become accustomed to…material things…

If I honestly look at this scenario, the family unit is going through tough times…and will continue to…until at least a few changes are made. The dollar is our master…and because of it, we have or may end up with many physical, mental, emotional, financial, and spiritual problems. Is it really worth it?

I leave you with a thought!

I Leave You With A Thought.

Father: 1st generation...1900-1925
I'm sure glad the sun is setting...
I'm totally exhausted...as are the rest.
This homesteading certainly is no fun.
Hard work, and more hard work.
Winter is coming quick, and so much to do...
Finish the log house, gather firewood,
can some food, slaughter a cow for meat,
find enough hay/feed for the animals.
Thank God I have family close by...
If nothing else, they're a big support.
I'll rig up the old cutter and calèche
with the little stove...for the cold winter.

Son:
This is crazy, all I seem to be is a slave.
I know I'm complaining...but, someone has to...
I realize that we all have to work together,
but it would be nice to go visit neighbors...
especially that sweet young lady teacher.
I guess I'd better get back to work...
stop this day dreamin'...but, she is pretty.
I wonder if I can find the courage to ask her
to go to the harvest supper, I hope so...
Back to work...Dad's giving me that look...
I can't wait to get my own piece of land.
Things will be way different than his ways.

Father:
I know the boy think this is no fun, rightly so...
but, that's life. I wish I could give him more,
and perhaps, if we all work hard together,
we may be able to procure more homestead land...
That's probably the best I can do for him.
It isn't much, yet it'll give him a chance
to get started...I hope he'll appreciate
my reason to prod...life's damn tough to survive.
I know my son has his eye on that young filly...
It's time he settles down, raises a family.
A heck! Back to work! There's so much to do...
break land, pull roots, harrow and disc...Ahhh!

Father: 2nd generation...1925-1950
I thought things would be easier than my father,
and, really, our lives have improved noticeably.
Our little town has all the basics that we need...
We thank God for church, credit, and neighbors.
We are fortunate...there's a one room school...
and, the kids are able to go most times...
depending if the crops are threshed and stooked.
We were lucky...we only lost one son, at birth.
The mid-wife was caught in a blizzard...
Hate to admit to this, but dad was so right...
We certainly have to work hard just to live.
Money is so scarce...Thank God the farm provides.

Son:

This is crazy, all I seem to be is a slave.
Farming is for the birds...too much work...
I'm gonna go to school...get some education,
move to a bigger center and find something better.
Sure we have food, clothes and shelter...
but, that Depression hurt many...pretty scary...
Being younger, these patched up hand-me-downs
were fine...no more...and the heatless two bedroom
leaky roof shack has got to go. No privacy!
Good thing I met this really sweet gal.
Her life is so similar to mine...and she's cute.
Here we go again...Stupid cows have to be milked.

Father:

I use to complain at how inconsiderate my dad was...
I sure see things differently today...He gave morals,
and purpose ...plus values and a belief in God...
things I want to pass on in kind to my children
More people are moving into the surrounding district,
therefore more businesses, which means more choices...
things like tractors, model-A's, binders and cutters.
I can see my offspring, in time, selling this farm...
move to a bigger center, find an 8 to 6 job,
or invest their meager savings into a small business.
If they devote alike hours as we did on this farm...
I know their material rewards will be a lot better.

21

Father: 3rd generation…1950-1975
Well, World War 2 changed most peoples lives…
Mine certainly did…Married my lovely sweetheart,
fought the Nazis, seen lots of terrible carnage,
got wounded enough to come home. I was fortunate.
I applied and got me a War Veteran's Loan…
very little interest charge and small payments.
We bought a small business in a large center.
The hours we put in are similar to the farm…
On the farm, we lived off what the land provided.
In the city we live off what our business creates…
so we are working very hard…soon it'll be ours…
to pass on to our son…for his material gains.

Son:
This is crazy, all I seem to be is a slave.
Have to work after school and every week-end…
plus, after hours…wash floors, stock shelves…
I have no time for sports or girlfriends…
Thinking about it, Dad pays very little anyways.
All he does is yell and scream…I hate it.
He expects respect…well I want respect too…
I have rights…I want, at least, minimum wage.
All my friends have cars and a chick beside them…
all except me…I can't wait to get on my own.
Man, I'm gonna get all the flashy clothes,
a neat car, spend lots of money…I can't wait!

22

Father:
I went to war to fight for liberty and freedom...
for independence...not dictatorship and fear...
Looking around me, I don't like what I'm seeing.
It seems we are giving control to our children...
We want to give our son a better life than we had,
but, what is better? Hippies? Drugs? Free Love?
I don't think so! He wants choices and free will.
Fine, if he uses his mind, not mind altering drugs...
Because material wealth is becoming so prevalent,
we're losing the battle on tradition...on family wealth...
and he's just about lost his spiritual wealth..
Thinking back...this wasn't what I fought that war for.

Father: 4th generation...1975-until today
I was so happy to leave home, to discover my life...
I wanted no commitments...just a good time...
My life-style was the source for my traveling,
and fortunately, I was always able to find work.
The material world was it...nothing else mattered.
I spent more than I made...and cared less...
To maintain this pace...plus my alcohol and drugs...
I relied a lot on lying, cheating, and stealing.
Finally, after many unwise, stupid decisions,
my behavior had to change drastically...and fast...
Luckily, I met this neat gal...and we married...
She helped me see light from a different angle.

23

Son:
>
> This is crazy, all I seem to be is a slave.
> All these menial tasks I'm expected to do...
> and if I slack off, life is not jolly...no siree.
> Mom and dad are trying to save my soul again...
> Why do Crusaders use the guilt trip approach?
> Good luck! How can something I can't see help?
> I know...dad's afraid I'll get into trouble...like him...
> I won't...I only smoke pot...and a bit of meth...
> if I need a boost...Better than a crack-head...
> Well, if I want to get some money for tonight,
> I'd better do these stupid, useless jobs...or else...
> This little hottie indicated she wants to see me.

Father:
This world is changing so much...and so fast,
yet, upon looking at these changes, much I question...
My grand-parents sought better living conditions
for their children, as did my parents for me.
I'm not so sure that following this tradition
is the right thing to do...There are so many false gods...
and, money heads that list as the true ruler.
A lot are enticing their children's love with possessions...
material chattels...When looking at the word "morals"...
ethical, honest, decent...many have become immoral...
What chance does my son have of being successful,
emotionally and spiritually, the things that really count?
In his life, many changes needed to occur for this to happen.

I Worry about Not Worrying...

Worry...Everybody worries...Right? I'm positive everyone has worried at certain times in their lives. But if you really think about it, worrying does absolutely nothing to facilitate any situation. You're wasting your time. First, it doesn't matter how much you worry about anything, it doesn't change a thing...nor make things better. Second, you may think you have a certain amount of control...You have no control at all over any type of worry. Third, usually what you think is going to happen on certain issues ...your reason for worry...normally is a lot less dramatic than what you imagined. Fourth, by worrying you are living in the future...and by living in the future you are missing the real life...Now!

I'd be a liar if I stated I never worry, but I can honestly say I've learnt to worry less, a lot less...The question I ask today is:" What's the worst thing that could happen to me?" By truly answering that question honestly, I am able to deal with the worst possible thing that I can imagine will happen...then get on with my real life today, not letting my mind go back there anymore. It's not easy, but by perseverance I will, can and do succeed.

Why choose this title? There are people like this...they worry about everything...I mean everything...and if they're not worrying...they're worrying about not worrying. They don't want to change... even though they can... all because of fear. They really know nothing else. They are missing out on living a challenging, intriguing life. Instead of letting others control their thoughts and actions...they would be the ones in charge. Makes sense to me. Guilt and worry, the two intimate buddies...One is the past, one the future, and both totally useless. Enjoy life on life's terms...It causes less worry!

I Worry About Not Worrying...

I think I'm going to worry today...Why not?
I've got lots to be concerned about...If only you knew!
     My kids could become a problem...what to do?
     It scares me when I think of their future....
     With all the rapes and murders...I'm quite alarmed.
My health seems to be sliding a bit...I might die...
After I'm gone, what will people say? That bothers me,
and, my poor helpless wife...what'll she think?

I have so much more to worry about...let me see...
Truthfully, I'll need at least the rest of this day...
     Well...hospitals are quite sick...they need help,
     yet, the wisdom of the government is to privatize.
     Great for the rich...but what about poor me?
With my wages, I could end up on social assistance...
Like a boat shrouded in a fog...I see no end in sight...
I'm so tired...It's tough trying to solve this dilemma.

I'm starting to feel nauseous, guessing what's in the future.
Phew! Problems! How will I find time to mull over them?
     I look at my stack of bills...and I shudder...
     It's never ending. Insurances, taxes, utilities,
     credit card expenses, mortgage and loan payments...
and I haven't even started on the important ones...
nourishment, clothes, vehicle, health, education...
I can't be bothered with recreation...people would laugh.

26

I feel a lot of guilt about incidents in my past...
and that bothers me...for, they could happen again.
I'm always fearful of what people think and say.
I'm a nice guy...once they get to know me...
but, I'm always apprehensive meeting new people.
I'm usually concerned if what I do is okay...
So, to make sure...I tend to stay in the background...
that way I have some control...and I worry less.

I remember once, when I was a kid, peeing my pants
in class. Everybody taunted me...I was so embarrassed...
I promised myself never would that happen again...
Similar to a brand searing my skin, marking me
for life...I have never forgotten, nor will I...
To achieve this, I make darn sure I'm the director,
thought it's tough being both the puppet and manipulator...
so I worry...afraid I might not do a proper job.

Why am I thinking about that when life's passing me by?
At this rate it don't matter...the whole world is crazy...
People using God as their excuse to kill and maim.
I wrestle with the fact that God should intervene...
Even though He's given us free-will and choices.
I often wonder if there's still room left in His Garden...
and that causes anxiety attacks...fearing the worse,
because I'm not sure if I'll even get to paradise...Ouch!

27

I look out my window…and the sun is shining…
I can already hear it…the weather's killing the crops…
       The poor farmer will complain…as he always does…
       Most do well…I mean, look at the equipment, the land…
       Got to have money to afford all those expenses.
What about us city folk? We're stuck holding the bag…
And, really…Who Cares? I get all my meat at Safeway,
which is a better deal than buying from those cry babies…

I think I've digested a lot of issues today…
many of which I've rehashed countless times before.
       I'm at the point where I worry about worrying…
       Insanity is doing the same thing over and over…
       expecting different results…That's me all right.
Guilt spotlights the past…Worry underlines the future…
and I'm stuck dead center…living in both worlds...
understanding neither, yet seeking that illusive answer.

I worry what will happen when the full moon appears…
therefore, I'd better get my act together, and…

Everyone Dies...Yet, Not Everyone Has Lived...

Bernie was my friend...Oh sure, he was family...but foremost he was a friend. I really knew Bernie in his younger years, when I would spend some time on the farm in Jackfish, Saskatchewan, or he would come and visit us in North Battleford. He always treated me with respect...and for that I thank him.

Bernie came from an athletic family. His brothers...and there was seven of them... all played sports...especially hockey. Bernie was the most athletic of that bunch. At an early age he had been spotted by The Montreal Canadiens, and he became part of their system.

Bernie met Claudette. They were such a good match, very compatible. They married quite young. He ended up in the Eastern USA playing hockey, starting a family...and moving to many different cities. After many years, he finally closed his hockey career and became an R.C.M.P. Just by the number of officers in and out of uniform, at his funeral...I would have to say he was well respected by his peers. Many tears were shed by his fellow workers.

Bernie is no longer with us, yet his spirit lives in so many hearts. Bernie was no saint...Bernie was human, but what he took from life he returned many times over. Bernie was my friend....He lived life to the fullest...What more can you ask?

Bernard Blanchette: 1947-2006...Died August 25, 2006

Everyone Dies...Yet, Not Everyone Has Lived...

Death begins at birth...
with life passing by in a flash...
then we return to the earth...
mostly in the form of ash...
Everyone...everyone dies...
It matters not...foolish or wise...
for...choices He did give...
Alas...not everyone has *really* lived...

History states..."To predict the future...
study the past. It repeats itself
time and again...after short intervals."
We should learn from our good deeds...
and from our failures and mistakes.
Most people do...Governments don't.

If one studied Bernie's history, his past...
without a doubt...sports would be the catalyst,
the means that resolved his worth...his value...
Claudette was number one...that was a given...
but so was hockey, so was golf, so was fishing.
One belief he always kept:" To yourself be true."

In keeping with Bernie's past, another example
was his three children...They were the apple
of his eye...So much love...and just mention
the little ones...His smile...a ray of tenderness,
filled with a real passion and true devotion.
If nothing else, they relieved most of his stress.
In life, you always pursue to succeed...

30

but, first you must deal with disappointments.
You learn how to thrive through failures...
It's important to always count your successes,
and, not to be concerned with your setbacks.
In glancing back...we become winners, not losers.

Bernie had some very interesting careers...
and because of his choices, there was much fear...
fear of threatening injuries, fear of death...
Drafted by The Montreal Canadiens, he began
his hockey journey...unsure of where he would land.
This was a tough physical, demanding, grueling life...

After a long period of professional hockey,
he'd had enough. Time for a new vocation...
Though not an enforcer during his hockey career,
he became one upon joining the RCMP.
He had an eagerness...actually a real passion
for this calling...earning him much respect.

Life being a challenge, did exactly that...
Thought he liked his work, other passions burned...
so into business he went...A lesson was learnt.
Most people think being in business is a scheme
to get rich...Bernie proved this to be a fallacy.
Lucky him...The door to the RCMP was still open...

Everyone has been granted the gift of perception...
but, many don't realize they have this power...
Power of observation, of insight, of acuity...
the power of sensitivity...especially towards others.
Thought will justify...the heart tells the truth.
Many go with the mind... contravening what is right...

One trait of Bernie's was to study people...
to observe...He was a great judge of character.
He had much compassion...a real understanding...
He felt that without contradictions and conflict,
achieving harmony or resolutions was impossible...
He rarely provoked, yet he rarely backed down.

Bernie had many friends...people he valued...
He was the type who was in-tune with himself,
therefore, being in the spotlight wasn't important.
In fact, he felt comfort being in the background,
helping and supporting others in their quest
to achieve the praise he didn't want, nor desire.

One day, Bernie didn't feel well, so he went to the doctor...
They told him he had a tumor, and the prognosis
wasn't good...Now was the time to settle accounts...
decide priorities...make amends...clean the slate...
Also, talk of his fears...the unknown...his concept of God,
yet, listen to the fears and pain of his loved ones.

Bernie loved Claudette...there was never a doubt...
He respected and cherished her values, her standards...
Her and the kids gave him a purpose to live...fully...
As his physical strength faded, his spiritual hunger
increased...He wanted life, but death wasn't a fear...
He knew his frailties...He also knew God loved him.

Bernie knew the parable of Jesus knocking on the door...
waiting for a response...The door knob was on his side...
For Bernie there was only one choice...open the door...
which he did. Jesus humbly entered Bernie's spirit,
felt very much at peace...then advised Bernie
that his journey on earth had come to an end.

Why God chose Bernie to live...we'll never know...
Why He gave him these particular challenges...
again, we'll never know...But does it matter?
Bernie had fulfilled the roles he'd been given...
with dignity, merit, respect and love.
His mental presence shrouds those closest to him.

Did Bernie live his life to the fullest?
I would say yes...based on observation of others.
Family is biased...Often the truth gets twisted.
The gauge I would have to use to conclude this...
are his friends, his colleagues, his neighbors...
Their stories...their memories...their admiration,
their esteem...are the true measure of Bernie's worth.

When I look up to the stars and the Milky Way...
I wonder if you're up there somewhere,
smiling your smile...piercing blue eyes watching...
Your image will be remembered in love by many.
Thank-you Bernie for being a leader, an example...
But most of all thanks for being my friend...Take Care!

Whatever You Hope For, I Hope It's Enough...

All around me people are getting out of a relationship, and back into one just as fast. They've not had time to sift through the rubbish of the previous relationship, trying to understand why it dissolved...then bringing this same waste into the next relationship expecting different results...This is what got me thinking. I figured I'd try and understand what 'relationship' meant to me...if I was out to lunch or what. I was curious, therefore I decided to write about it...

Relationships today...at least more so today...are a real mishmash of combinations...Male/male, female/female, male/female, two males/one female, two females/one male...and the list goes on...Is this better? Does this control sexual diseases? Does this give stability and morals to the children, or help them in their own sexual identification...for there are always children? What does love truly mean? Is having only a physical relationship better than the whole package... which includes intimacy? As far as I'm concerned, these are important questions, and yes I do have my personal feeling about all of this...

I care not who you are, each and everyone of us wants happiness, wants joy, wants fulfillment in this life. I've been trying not to make too many judgment calls as to people's preferences, for I have no right in denouncing people for their choices. Each person has the right...and duty...to choose their life-style. In whatever life style you choose, and whatever you wish for on your path in life, I truly hope it's enough

Whatever You Hope For, I Hope It's Enough...

Often a relationship doesn't make much sense...
Two people with such different backgrounds,
using masks and pretence to try and impress.
Moods are like a lightening rod...up and down...
That's life...You become what you've experienced...
Sometimes you're floating, sometimes you feel drowned.

You enter something...With no clue of where you're at...
where you're heading, how far it is, when it'll end...
Still, you set out...making wrong turns...getting mad,
then wonder why this plan doesn't work...again...
Only then do you ask the questions that make you react...
Relationships is life...and life is an incessant problem...

Why is it you often seek the approval of others?
You can't live someone else's dreams and visions...
and why should you! Use others to discuss, to confer...
then, go with your heart. That's your only option...
You must have faith in your preference of a partner...
If there's doubt, use others insights in your decisions.

The world seems to promise so much, yet that pledge
can be deceiving, misleading...because world means people...
Conditions don't make you who you are, but the courage
to reveal what you are...and that's part of the whole...
A union of two doesn't need an orator on stage,
making promises, wittingly destroying the others soul...

Taking care of your inner needs is so important...
especially when in a non-traditional union.
Each person...no matter the style...mustn't plant
doubt. Thoughts and emotions must be agreed upon.
Only when this occurs...the outer needs shan't
be denied. They'll be provided because of this bond.

We do many stupid things to gain a reputation,
to gain an identity...Being young is part of this craze...
Some never grow-up...or tire of self-gratification.
Tell me! Why give life to a child...to nurture, to raise...
To Teach...if your mirror incessantly displays aberration?
They need love; they need direction; they need praise...

Whatever you hope for, I hope it's enough...
Make sure your higher power's name is not yours...
for you may believe you're all powerful and tough...
Just think! Your actions may become part of the lore,
of the wisdom...of what not to do to attain love...
Together, seek your Higher Power...Life will then soar...

Moving across the borders of your mind...in flight...
chasing a hope, a wish, a desire...chasing a dream...
asking the rhetorical question: "Is this choice right?"
Arriving at truth through deductions, you feel serene...
at least somewhat...yet, you must appreciate plight...
There are so many undercurrents in life's streams.

Swept Away By The Stroke of Time...

I find time passing at such a speed, changes happening every day. The computer has changed everything. Communication is a split second away...I ask myself quite often, "do we really need all of this?"

Everything today is so impersonal...Unfortunately many people fit into that category. We don't take the time, nor do we have the time to know the people around us...we're too busy. Businesses are open seven days a week, 12 hours per day. Man and his wife hardly communicate, and the children...often...take care of themselves. A family outing is trudging and bumping alone in some mall, ending it by visiting a Fast Food Take-Out, enjoying a cholesterol filled hamburger and fries...Such a treat. A great place to have a conversation that has substance.

I guess I'm a bit of a nostalgia type...I remember in my youth, how we had time...for family, for friends, for neighbours. We had so much more trust of people, of the system... Today, all we have left are memories... The rest has all been swept away by the stroke of time.

The town I use in this poem is fictional, though I could probably name a few in similar situations...and I do know these particular towns are really, really struggling.

That's call progress...

Swept Away By The Stroke Of Time...

Coming home after many years, I couldn't believe the changes.
What a shock! My vibrant little town was mostly a ghost...
The buildings...the ones that remained...were mostly toast...
Where'd everyone go? Everything seems so strange.
Walking down main street, I notice all the broken signs...
Sitting on the bench besides "Jonesy's," I got lost in time...

Opening the door, a little bell broke the silence...
ting, ting, ting. "Hey, Johnnie! How're you young man?"
"Real good, Mr Jones. Mom wants something condense...
milk...I think...Please put it on the bill. Oh! and some jam."
He was a kind, old gent...and truly a friend...
He always meant what he said...There was no pretend...

"Johnnie, are you playing ball this coming season?"
"Not sure, might have to work...You heard about the mill?"
"Yah! People'll need support...Did you hear the reason?"
"According to dad...someone was messin' with the till...
Lot's of money missin'...no insurance...and now, no jobs.
I hope they find that critter...It just ain't right to rob."

Walking out of our little corner grocery store,
I looked down the main street, and I sighed...
I knew everyone, and they all waved and said "Hi."
Such a friendly little town, even though it was poor.
Walking down the dusty sidewalk, I felt comfort...
The businesses were going to provide our support.

Looking around, there was a lot of bustle...
A few had stopped to chat by the little bakery...
Others were smiling, but you knew they had much worry.
For me to piece it was too much of a puzzle.
I headed towards my next stop...Mr. Davidson's,
the local hardware that had everything...bar none...

38

Getting up, I hear a voice in the background...
I see Mrs. Cooper...Wow! Has she ever aged...
I've known her forever...she was always so sage,
so astute. "Hi, Mrs. Cooper, where you bound?"
"Nowhere John, I'd like to join you in stride.
Remember Davidson's? The place you kids use to hide?"

Lanterns hanging from the rafters, guns on the wall...
The smell...sawdust on the creaky wooden floor...
Different sized snares and traps placed in their stalls...
and, all those modern gadgets ...I just love this store.
I eyed my glove... It was still here...my good luck...
Yah right! Not unless Upstairs helped...Life sucked!

"Johnnie! Good to see you...How yah bin? What's new?"
"Hi Mr. Davidson, I come to pick-up a few nails...
Mom asked if I could charge? She home with the flu."
"Sure...What size do you need?" "For two inch rails."
"How's yur pa feelin' about the mill? Bad, I s'pect."
"Yah! Someone has to pay...He heard they're to inspect."

Walking out, I noticed Tommy's '57 Chevy...
and lucky him...all the chicks wanting his attention...
He acts as if he couldn't be bothered...All pretension.
What a jerk! Without the car where would he be?
There weren't many I tried to evade...He was one...
Even his mom, I'm sure, wonders "where'd he come from."

Heading towards Douglas Drugs, I hear my name...
"Johnnie! Have you heard the latest? They caught the thief."
"Hi Jane...Who?" "That new guy from the city...Steve..."
"Really! I'da thought it was that growly one...Mr. Lane..."
" Banker Billie noticed a lot of money in his account,
so, he made the company aware. That's how he was found."

"Remember the fire, after that Steve fella robbed the mill?
That was the beginning of the end for this little town.
Not long after that, Tommy got drunk and drowned...
Then Stan Douglas passed on. I still owe him a bill."
Walking past his shop, I looked in the cracked window.
I could picture him...talking to himself, walking real slow.

Mr. Douglas was older than Adam...He just had to be...
His face was so wrinkled, it looked like a road map...
but, a fantastic pharmacist...He knew it all...from A to Z...
Looking up, a big, full smile displaying a wide gap,
where his teeth had once been. "How can I be of service?
Who's sick? Your mom? What's she need? Show me the list."

Waiting while he got what mom wanted, I walked around...
Another store I just loved...Just like it's owner...unique...
To the candy counter my forlorn nickel was bound...
making me come with it...of course...Gum's what it seeked.
"Johnnie! Your moms prescription's ready. Thanks...take care..."
One more stop before heading home...Mike's Men's Wear.

This store still had the hitching rail to tie horses...
and, for the odd cowboy...this was his only means...
Walking in, the pervasive smell of leather was very keen.
"Hi Mike. Hey's that the latest edition of 'The Source'?
Anything on the mill? No? Can I charge some gloves?
Probably get summer work if push comes to shove."

Walking out, I remembered I had one more place to go...
The wooden sidewalk creaking with each step I took,
I had to stop at one of my favourites " To Take Time Books."
Harper Lee's *"To Kill A Mockingbird"* was 'a novel in the know...'
according to the reviews, and Triple T's had it on display.
"Your moms credit is good"...I was hoping they would say...

40

"Hey, I don't believe it...Mike's is still open.
Hi Mike! How are you? Remember me? Johnnie?
Man! You look great...Tell me...what's the key?"
"Don't look too close, Johnnie...there's lots of pretend."
Looking at me, sadly smiling, he gives me a sigh...
"Next month I'm closing...Time to say good-bye."

Mom was walking around, though she should have been in bed.
"It sounds like they caught the culprit, Dad'll be happy...
How come you're still up? You look half dead...
I picked up a new paperback from Triple T's."
The phone rang. "Johnnie! The mill's on fire...come quick."
"Mom! Mill's on fire...Probably some fool playing tricks."

It lasted all night...The sole fire truck ran out of water.
Everything...Everything was lost...Nothing could be saved...
For most, the mill was their soul...it was now their grave.
All had lost their security...including my father.
Most vented their frustrations by blaming Steve...
Faulty wiring was the cause. No one wanted to believe...

Dad found the odd jobs...I helped a little...
Mom could squeeze a nickel out of a penny...
We survived...not well...but more than many.
We had a strong faith to help us with life's riddles.
After a time, I had to leave...to start my own life...
Thanks to my life experiences, I learnt to survive.

Reaching the end of my walk, I feel a sadness...
It all seem to be swept away by the stroke of time.
All that's left is mem'ries...Reality is not kind...
The simpler years are gone...no more. That's progress...
Taking one last look, for I don't suspect I'll be back,
I walk to my car parked beside the abandoned tracks.

41

Peeking Through The Looking Glass.

In this poem I'm trying to find and correctly place some of the many pieces in my personal puzzle. All of these pieces concern where I've been and where I'm at. To do this I must understand I can't live in my past, yet I must review my past, for it is my link to this day.

This is a poem about me and some of my issues...how they affect me, and from there decide what I want to keep and what I want to change...To make that sort of decision I needed to peek through the looking glass...a very interesting study...After having had a chance to see, to question, then to decide the fate of the emotion, the thought, the feeling...was quite an exercise. Of course I chose to change some of my thoughts and feelings... to take a different path...a change of attitude.

I was able to find the correct places for a few of the pieces in this mixed-up puzzle...That's something!

Peeking Through The Looking Glass.

My Mirror...a contemplation of diverse images,
layered through so many different stages...
all presented by direct, explicit messages.
In my mind, I start flipping through the pages,
trying to comprehend these directives, to gauge
a pattern discerning the route to take. This passage,
from thought to action, flows throughout my ages,
understanding my loves...understanding my rages,
and things in-between...My journey originates...

In trying to determine why I do the things I do,
I'm checking to see who're all the folks in my pew.
My parents, grandparents, uncles, aunts...What a zoo!
All had an opinion, yet most didn't have a clue
of what I needed...nor did I! I lived their behaviours.
The turmoil that I recognize today have been stored
in my soul's vault...with their names on it. Now, that door
is slowly creeping open, letting me see more and more.
My parents had the strongest impact, that's for sure...
thanks to my grandparents, who had been taught the same lore.

Peeking through the looking glass, I look around,
noticing the private sectors of my soul. My heart pounds.
My thoughts I've experienced, but not all the sounds,
not all the words. I feel that emotion fear get me down.
Whatever's happening in my outer world I can see,
but that inner place just wants to make me flee.
I am what I've lived, therefore this is whom I'll be...
if I do not change...But, I do want to, actually.
What a paradox! I'm afraid to question honestly,
for, I'm not sure I can answer all truthfully...

43

My siblings and I were normal…arguing and fights.
Eventually, dad would have to scream and get uptight.
If we didn't quit, he'd smack us with a lot of might…
and in the corner we'd go…crying…what a sight!!
Today…as adults…we have gained some undercurrents…
though there are none of us who are belligerent.
Actually, with them I'm lucky! I've so little to vent…
yet, they know of my current anger and resentments…
and, in most cases they are bias, which is gallant,
but is this my remedy? No! But I still love their intent.

When mom died, it left a long lasting impression.
Dad always needed control, which caused much contention.
He loved me, but used the wrong tools in his lessons.
Soon after mom's death, he went into a depression…
alcohol became his companion, his soul mate.
I was born with this gene addictions…I just couldn't wait
to escape, sardonically to find myself using the same bait
as he. I was lured, thinking this was a good trait,
believing this was part of my lot, my destiny, my fate.
Today, I understand why I had an overflowing plate…
My life was an impulse, lots of things I couldn't relate,
even though I wanted to follow what was on his slate.

Who so is more a reflection of my parents
then me, their child. My role models had no patent,
except that my dad was much an autocratic gent…
In most cases, his word was the rule…Not much bend…
I promised myself I'd never be like that…
yet, I am…in spite of wearing many different hats
in raising my kids. I truly know not where I'm at.
I feel like I'm in a maze, I feel like I'm in a trap.
Unfortunately, this has caused me a lot of wrath…

When it comes to friends…I really don't have a lot.
Too many aided my dilemma, of which I fought.
Those whom I've let in do challenge my thoughts,
and that's important, for many lessons have been taught.
Acquaintances…sure they're part of the bigger picture.
Like any nature painting, the trees are permanent fixtures…
it's a nice setting, a bit of tone…but, merely gesture.
These folks hardly caused me problems, that's for sure.
No! It was "my good buddies…the enema couriers"
that caused me my grief…pretending to be my cure.

I mustn't forget my past lovers, nor my ex-spouse…
remembering the facts, not solely to arouse
my testosterone, causing a flame I'll have to douse.
In this solitary revelation, I need to browse
deeply and honestly about how I truly feel.
My emotions, my passions, I'd better not conceal,
searching for truth, knowing I can't make a deal…
If I'm not candid, my wounds just won't heal.
In all honesty…some of these mem'ries I won't yield.
The play-backs are to important, too good, too real.

As a child I encountered emotional misuse,
and as a parent I've handed out this same abuse.
I tell myself, I am powerless, that's my excuse.
I must change…my poor kids…all I do is accuse.
They are not an extension of me, but an end in itself.
To make this happen, I can give them a lot of wealth…
mental, emotional, spiritual…things that are felt.
To make this change, a new hand needs to be dealt.
First, I need to come to terms with my past self.

45

It's easy to talk the talk...but to walk the walk,
it takes someone who has knowledge of the knocks...
humbling experiences. At times, I turn back the clock,
wondering, thinking, feeling...probing my inner thoughts.
I can still recall as a child many emotions...
some were quite joyful, leaving lasting impressions,
yet, there were many filled with angry words spoken.
I grasp today how this has affected my opinions...
A lot of mixed messages, a lot of confusion...
Is it any wonder I felt my life had no real direction?

I am wise enough to know that I am fallible,
that I've made lots of mistakes and capable
of many more. Two emotions that I need to dispel,
to drive away, are fear and anger...while I'm still able.
If I could rein in those emotions, put on the brakes,
I know for sure that I'd have a lot less heartaches.
To gain prowess and patience would help me stake
a claim on my future...today...not 'I can't make it.'
I'm slowly learning...At times I give...at times I take.
Nothing to it. A walk in the park, a piece of cake...Dream on!

In remembering my disease...someone with an addiction...
I need to be very concerned of contradictions,
yet, I seem to thrive on this...and also contention...
arguing, especially with my kids, and equivocation...
I do deceive, but less...I love doing things the hard way.
Looking into my past, the amount I've had to pay...
emotionally...has been high. I really hope some day
to be able to look at my past in a new ray.
To do this, I have to dig deeper into the clay...
my subconscious...and ask God to show me the way.

If God is to show me the way, then I need to ask
what is His will for me...not my will for me...my task...
I can't hide nothing from Him, so why keep the mask.
I suppose, if I really wanted, I could still bask
in the belief that I'm in control...God gives me free will.
Knowing what I know, defiance may give me a thrill,
and, supposedly God forgives even if I take a spill...
but, why continue on the path to be spiritually ill?
Makes no sense. I wonder what kind of spiel
awaits me...St. Pete's rhetoric...written in quill.

Did I really accomplish anything from this search?
I feel I have, but I also know I must encourage
myself to continue this pursuit. It'll take courage...
meaning I can't merely sit on my perch
pretending that all is fine...because it's not!
The closer I come to know me, and really I aught...
after all this emotional probing that I sought...
the more I realize how much I still have got
to learn. One thing for sure, I could never have bought
this knowledge...never...These lessons were all hard knocks.

What I've come to understand is...until I've resolved
issues from my past, and forgiven those involved...
only then will the healing begin...That's how it evolves.
My adult self...my thinking self...must truly devolve
to my emotional self... my childlike self... that change
is in order. Past negative feelings will be exchanged
with positive awareness, yet making sure not to derange,
destabilize my thoughts without knowing how to arrange
the new process. If done properly, I'll have a whole range
of choices. That's what I want and need...Is that strange?

47

Annoyance With A Capital "A"

Do you ever get mad and frustrated with so many of these "User Friendly" companies...like utilities companies...or banks...or telemarketers ...or telephone companies? Of course there are dozens more that I could vent my frustration...and I do, when I'm in contact with them...companies like lawyers, dentists, accountants (though our accountant truly tries to get us the best deal)...so maybe not accountants...as much. Of the trades mentioned...they're not all bad...don't get me wrong, but there are a lot of bad ones amongst them. As government offices go, they have so much driftwood, subordinates and mandarins...people who are in charge...it's a wonder anything gets done.

I guess it's the philosophy of the company that dictates the workers attitude...and most big corporations want big profits and really could care less about service and all that entails...That costs money...so cut back on staff. Instead of 15-20 or more people, cut it down to 1 or 2...or better yet...let some machines do this service work.

It really has become a dilemma...'a situation involving choice between equally unsatisfactory alternatives.' On the one hand , what they call 'service' is nearly non-existent...at least in my eyes...and on the other hand, that's all we have to work with, and it's not getting any better...so we have to use the 'service' they feel so exuberant to give us. The end result: We are getting a whole lot less and it's costing us a whole lot more. I've always been one who is wary of getting shafted... and for the most part, this is exactly what is happening. To me it's not right...As an individual, these corporations could care less what I think...I get so frustrated...

Annoyance With A Capital "A"

<u>To irritate</u>: *To annoy, to exasperate...*
These adjectives express well my feelings...

Banks Annoy me...with a capital "**A.**"
Bank's advertisements make them look so good...
yet, at the end of the day...it leaves a bad taste.
They want to invest my money for their gain...
How do they thank me for lending them my money?
They benefit me .025% interest on my savings...
yet, charge me at least 8% if I need to borrow.
The features I truly appreciate the most...
When I make a deposit, they charge me a fee!!
For every cheque I write...another charge!!
and the one I really like...The overdraft fee...
Often, living becomes a struggle, so friends help...
The bank, being my friend, wants to facilitate.
How you ask? By charging me double digit interest..
A true friend! In all honesty, they're not alone...

<u>To infuriate</u>: *To enrage, to make your blood boil...*
These adjectives express well my feelings...

Utility Companies Annoy me...with a capital "**A.**"
I'm thinking incompetence has to be the reason...
"All our agents are currently busy...For assistance
please stay on line... <u>Your call is very important to us.</u>
Your call may be monitored for 'quality assurance'."
I just feel like picking up the phone and chucking it.
I can picture myself chocking someone...just for relief...
Glancing at my bill, I swear...This is outright thieving...
Take my electricity bill...I understand current charges,
b..u..t...transmission chg, destination chg, local access fee...
plus a balancing pool allocation...Give Me A Break!!
Natural gas is not much better...A current charge,
then a delivery chg, a fixed chg...and a variable chg.

And I have no cause to be infuriated? Yah right!!
To some, stealing maybe a service...but, it's still a crime...
    <u>To aggravate</u>: *To frustrate, to fan the flames...*
    These adjectives express well my feelings...

Telemarketing Annoy me...with a capital **"A."**
I admire a foreigner who tries to speak my language,
and, I honestly do make an effort to understand...
Yet, for some nationalities...trying to speak English
is similar to gargling and talking at the same time...
A Catch-22...To practice their English, they need a job...
yet, few get hired, because of their fractured English...
Why do telemarketers usually choose this type?
What's the advantages...if people continually hang-up?
Sadly, ethnicity is a telemarketers best friend.
I've come to have no patience...for three reasons...
The product they're peddling, I'd rather not want nor need...
I hate being hood-winked by aggressive, deceptive people...
and I hate trying to decipher my own language.
By conversation's end, we're both totally frustrated.

    <u>To exasperate</u>: *To irritate, to drive around the bend...*
    These adjectives express well my feelings...

Telephone Companies Annoy me... with a capital **"A."**
They're in the same class as a utilities company.
These cheap a-holes, need a sexy automated voice...
a "phoney"...who has a vocabulary of about 80 words,
to 'prompt and direct' your call to the 'proper' station...
What ever happened to people talking to people...
interacting...Service was very essential ...Not anymore...
"<u>Your call is so important</u>, yet it maybe monitored...
To enhance your position, please stay on the line...
Your call will be answered in approximately 42 minutes..."
I try not to use expletive...but it's beyond my control...
They spew out of my mouth at an alarming rate...
as I bang the phone...I could just scream blue murder...
Becoming aware of my surroundings, I only hope
that no customer has witnessed this childish tantrum...
Unfortunately, a few have...Thank God they've had empathy...

Walking On Thin Ice...

I started out this poem with a whole different concept. I wanted to write about not taking the time to go see someone, especially an older person, usually a loved one. Why? Because it's always the coulda, woulda, shoulda...and before I quit procrastinating about going to visit, they die. I had a title chosen, everything. I started writing that poem, but, it didn't feel right...so I changed a line, then a verse, and before I realized it this was something completely different...so I focused on where I was going with this poem...I wasn't sure, but I just felt I had to write what I was writing... therefore, away I went...Got a new title too...

It's a story, something I made-up, yet looking further into this poem I see so much of me...in both the 1st and 2nd person. When my father was really sick, I approached him and made my amends to him. I wanted to do this before he passed on...Actually he died not long after that...But this is not his story, or anything close to it, and actually I hadn't even thought of that event while writing this poem. I mention it...only to remind me what it was like...the emotions, the feelings, the elation of having removed this rubbish...and to keep it as a reference if the occasion occurs again...and it has...more than once.

The lesson for me in this writing...There comes a time in everyone's life...because of sickness, because of age, because of choices, and the list goes on...when we truly have to examine our conscience...and in many cases there are amends that should be made...If we want to heal, a good house cleaning is the answer, and for me that meant a lot of humility to atone, or at least be willing to atone, for my wilful wrong doings .

Enjoy! To be honest, I'm still amazed that this particular poem came to be. That's the nice thing about this type and style of writing...I just follow the thoughts and quite often I will say," Where did that come from?" I just shake my head, and keep on writing.

Thanks to Andrea Klingspohn for this title...

51

Walking On Thin Ice...

We were buddies...I mean real soul-mates...
and together, some of the stuff we generated
was amazing ...at least that's how we felt.
With scrap lumber and rusty nails we created
a unique go-cart...Balloon tires, a seat of felt,
and a wobbly steering wheel held with a belt...
     He loved telling invented stories...
     and really...they seemed like true glory...

We determined we could drink and smoke
at thirteen...We stole equally from our folks...
Both boasting of conquests, we remained virgins...
yet, had graduated to marijuana and tokes.
He had to be careful, for he had delicate skin.
He shared his fears of death...That bothered him...
     Looking back, he was often quite sick...
     His body sure took the licks...

We took different paths...I had places to go...
yet, sometimes we'd meet, and the BS would flow...
My, he had changed, or perhaps it was me...
He never was a good liar...I sensed his sorrow...
The last time I saw him, he stated his knee
was sore...His eyes spoke of fear and worry.
     I felt sadness...I was sure why...
     and yet, I didn't want to pry...

One day I got a call from my friend's niece.
Life being what it is...the journey never ceases...
Her quivering, trembling voice made me shiver...
Her uncle had surrendered, and died in peace.
He ended up in a coma...He never really suffered...
She had found a letter for me...She wanted to deliver...
     I was curious what it would reveal...
     or what it would keep concealed...

A few days later someone called my name...
Turning, I notice this beautiful frame...
A blond coiffure, shapely legs and a wide smile.
The cheekbones and dimples...exactly the same.
We talked of her uncle...his life and his trials...
It just wasn't fair...all the pain he'd compiled...
A few tears slid down her cheek...
    A strong person, yet feeling so weak..
    My eyes...brimming...I felt very meek...

Taking the envelope, I hesitated...unsure...
This was his poker game...he was the dealer...
Looking at my cards, could I fold or continue?
Having had a choice, I feel I would've deferred,
but, the option wasn't mine, so I took my cue.
Opening the letter, I felt no regrets...no rue...
    I asked her to sit and wait...I insisted...
    Reading the first line, my eyes misted...

    I'm not certain if I still had you as a friend...
    My self-importance I really needed to tend.
    What a jerk! I shoulda shown my inner feelings...
    my affection...instead of being so disparaging...
    But no, my pride needed a self-promotion...
    I oughta been using feelings instead of emotions.
It wasn't what I did, but what I stopped doing,
that became the problem...Who was I fooling?
Only me...Life wasn't the problem...not at all...
but, living it properly was...I had to learn to crawl
before I walked...learn to listen so I could speak,
and discovered how to search for truths...to seek...
    As you know, things happen in life...That's life...
    Sometimes joy/sorrow... other times elation/strife.
    These feelings were usually caused by intimates...
    They knew which buttons...how to dangle bait...
    To understand what their motives represented,
    I needed to examine my role...what signs had I sent

53

During this period of time, my daughter was killed...
The pain...indescribable...I had no more will...
I wanted revenge, thought there was none to be had...
She took a dare while drinking... and drowned...So sad...
Talk about guilt...I took full responsibility.
Clearly, my life-style for her was a liability.

Looking around, there was Judy staring into space
"I recall your cousin" I said. "Such an expressive face...
When I heard...I really wanted to share his loss.
I truly tried to make contact...Not a trace..."
"Things were so bad, even the sun wouldn't cross
his street. He'd finally had enough...A total waste."
I finally did call him...we both cried...
He was so fried...My time I did bide...
By being honest, I became his guide...

Over the years I was mad at you...I don't know why!
I heard you were really hitting the rye...So was I...
You, at least, had the courage to quit...I couldn't...
The choices I made in my past, regrettably, wouldn't
let go...That's why I was mad...You were determined...
I was jealous, and afraid to ask where to begin...
I didn't want my past to catch me, so I ran...
I was a sick person, not a bad person...
I finally figured that one out...in a hospital...
Oh yah! My past caught up... big time...What a fall...
Memories... swirled around like a carousel.
Hope there's another path...I've already been to hell...
I've come to realize I made a lot of bad choices...
To justify, I blamed...An excuse to raise my voice.
I lost my wife, my daughter, my faith, my friends...
I wanted control, and didn't understand amends.
Pride nearly killed me...I finally got on my knees...
Today, I'm asking of your forgiveness...please...

Thinking about it...Life's like walking on thin ice...
Because of circumstances and conditions, his eyes
guided his soul...That wasn't always a good thing...
Life's undercurrent certainly didn't think twice
about his concerns...Who knew what it would bring?
He fought that current...Therefore he felt the sting...
    He fell through the ice....again and again ...
    never realizing the reason for this trend.

You know my friend, I really did suffer a lot...
No excuses...Anything coming through, I caught...
That was life... Why I was chosen, I never understood ...
therefore I was mostly angry...Nothing was good...
Have you ever hated? I did...I hated most people,
but, I hated me the most...I'd lost my soul.
    Today I've gained a bit of stability
    in my life...and a touch of humility...
    You know, I don't think less of me...not at all...
    I only think of me less...I finally hit the wall...
    At long last, I realize it's I who determines
    my worth, and not worry about concerns...

I had to stop for a moment... to digest...
Wow! He was putting a lot of issues to rest.
His was a honest, poignant account...emotive...
To repay for wreckage of his past...his quest
was his amends...This was his reason, his motive...
And, he was the first one that he had to forgive.
    Judy sat watching...playing with a string...
    gauging my thoughts, not missing a thing...

    I'm sure you're wondering why this letter.
    In death I want my side of the ledger
    clean...no regrets...I slandered you,
    I resented you...I'm sure you had many clues...
    I was jealous...You represented all I wanted.
    Thanks for the talks...I appreciate you not flaunting it.

I had a lot of good in my life...One concerns
our friendship...That wasn't hard to discern...
at least not for me...You knew me, you accepted me
for who I was. You taught me that nothing was free...
except a Higher Spirit...I changed because of you...
yet, I had to do it for me...That was the clue...
    I am so proud...I have finally found peace...
    My emotional pains are gone...they've ceased...
    At one time I thought we'd both be fried...
    So, if you could gain peace of mind...so could I.
    My purpose is to arrive at a spiritual life.

How? By arriving at truth...I've had enough strife
I know I won't be in this world much longer.
Though I am very weak...I feel so much stronger.
Think of me... from time to time... in memory...
I'm not afraid, but unsure of my next journey...
I'm human...At times, my mind plays games...
I'm hoping, with the love I feel...there's no flame.
    I'm just babbling on...I'm glad Judy brought
    you this letter. She is everything that I sought...
    I love her a whole lot...She has much empathy.
    She showed and gave a lot of compassion to me...
    Her take on life is very similar to yours...
    but...don't try and impress her with your lore.
You reading this letter means only one thing...
I might even be trying on a pair of wings...
Now, wouldn't that be different...Unconceivable...
and yet, laying here wondering...I find it feasible...
So long and thank-you...Until we meet again...
and, I'm positive we will...my precious friend...

A tear ran down my cheek...then another...
My throat was so dry, I drank some water.
I kinda knew this letter was going to be tough ...
He left me with the impression of being a potter
at his wheel...mould, shape, and then a buff...
finally, wondering if he'd truly done enough.
    I humbly forgave him...I also had no doubt,
    that he certainly was on the right route.

Is It Really Worth It?

The people who migrated and help build the towns and villages so many years ago, would be shocked today to see how their little settlement has expanded and grown, yet if they peeled away the surface, they'd be surprised to see that not all is well.

Small town businesses are facing some real big challenges today. The big mega store is such a draw...so big, so huge, with so much to choose from...it's hard not to want to go there. They have such a tremendous buying power. Just in Canada alone, they all have 100's of huge stores...plus the USA, South America, Europe, Asia, Africa...and God knows where else. Some of these companies are buying in the millions and more, of one item, where the small independent is merely buying 2-3 items...They often sell for cheaper than the little guy can even buy. Because of their incredible sales volume world-wide, they can afford to work on a small net profit...they still end up with a huge amount of money for their shareholders.

Now what can the local little village/hamlet store owner offer compared to this? A lot, actually... They have many specials where the prices are comparable...and in many cases even cheaper...How can they do this? With a smaller overhead, with the attitude of trying to serve the customer...not rob them...working on a small profit margin, they are able to compete. By giving friendly service... by making the customer feel valued... by really trying to help them get what they want...by searching for items in their catalogues. By taking the time to converse with them...and truly listen...By organizing events for their customers, and enjoying the event with them...by donating and advertising for local committees/charities.

For the big stores it's all about money and profits...Of course the little guy needs to make money to live too...but it's way more than just money... It's wanting to be an integral part of their community...being able to participate in making their community a comfortable place to live.

Is this enough? And the real question is "Is it really worth it?" If small communities are to continue...yes! The folks who make up the community are the ones who will decide if a small business is wanted in their hamlet or not...If not, over time, the chances of this community survival are quite slim, also...unfortunately...

Is It Really Worth It?

In today's society, being an independent businessman
takes a lot of courage…If looking at the customer count,
this perception may be true…Some feel a franchise
is a better choice. There is some truth to that assessment,
but only some… Individualism and freedom are gone…
Whatever the name…this store will be alike to all the others…
Because they target a specific group…choices are limited.
Perhaps owning a small business is a fools dream…
but, these fools are willing to invest in their community.

Experiencing small town shopping is unique…
especially if you're from a large community.
They often have the neatest eclectic merchandise…
things you normally wouldn't find in a city store.
The reason behind the diverse inventory is two fold…
More customers…Better selection of essential needs.
Often, because of a small population in their village,
there is a limited traffic volume to their business …

The ideal…Having a store with much variety,
well stocked…and, many people who buy a lot…
It does happen…unfortunately not often enough…
Small town commerce have become convenience stores…
Big centres have selection and lower prices…so they say…
Therefore, it's really worth a persons precious time…
and energy…to save maybe ten or so dollars…
Hell, with the price of gas near a dollar a litre…
It only costs thirty bucks to save ten…Great Savings!

Service is the key to most small business success…
Thank God for that, for there is very little…or none
in the Box Stores…Their excuse…help is hard to find…
True today…but they've always had limited staff…
therefore, their excuses really doesn't wash well.
The small guy is only too happy to ask you
if you need help…and mean it…If you're new
to his area, he'll make you feel right at home…

The nice thing about small town shopping…the staff
usually knows everyone. Often they are related…
or a long time friend…Frequently they talk of family,
their kids, or the latest, salacious news release…
The worker habitually knows what their friends like,
therefore, show them trinkets that often appeal.
Good employees are like fine wine… savour them…
appreciate them…They will draw people in for you.

> All merchants wonder why some people won't shop
> locally…and when they do, it's so very little.
> I guess many feel the little guy has nothing to offer…
> Yet, when money becomes scarce, and they need help…
> who do they come to? You guessed it…The local keeper…
> Having no money left, many will ask if they can charge,
> and, in some cases, the owner complies…So accommodating…
> Unfortunately, payment usually takes a long time coming…

If a customer is loyal…they'll get good buys…
Often a small business's prices are a better deal
than 'the big boys'…Less overhead costs…although
the cost of the item is, no doubt, a lot higher.
They buy by the hundreds…he buys individually…
yet, he's willing to work on a smaller profit margin.
At the end of the day, he feels his conscience is clear…
He did his best to satisfy each and every customer…
He didn't always succeed, but the effort was there.

> In many cases, the small business is the pulse
> of the area. They spearhead many activities…
> With the cooperation of other local businesses…
> they advertise, they donations, they coordinate
> special functions…designed to help the community.
> The customers are their friends and neighbours…
> so, let them have fun, yet, help make the town attractive.
> It helps promote business, and people appreciate deeds…

Yet, on the other hand, if the local guy didn't do this,
or the local Chamber of Commerce didn't get involved...
in most cases, there would be very little local leisure activity.
The rationale is...many villages reverted to hamlet status...
for numerous reasons ...the biggest being, allegedly less taxes...
which, many beg to differ...The County grades roads,
collects garbage, reads water meters and collects taxes...
Local clubs and businesses are the Social Conveners.

One big dilemma many small businesses face,
is organizations wanting donations for their cause.
Without too much qualm, a businessman will support
the clubs that support him...But, the majority of demands
come from clubs that do very little...or no business locally...
The one that retailers despise...is when a local society
asks for money donations...then has the audacity to
buy at mega stores...never considering the local guy.
Talk about resentment...That is the ultimate insult...

Because of the change in attitude of the clientele...
Many small stores feel they must stay open
late, and work seven days a week...to compete...
This means more staff, yet with the labour laws
dictating stringent fines if not abided correctly,
the owner, often, ends up working these extra hours.
To make these few extra dollars, he gives up so much
valuable family time...and eventually his health...
Is this material gain worth the physical strife?

The businessman feels success when a profit is made...
mostly because of circumstances and a measure of luck...
If they think it's because of self...they really are the fool...
Even though they have knowledge, hard work and dedication,
if conditions are not right...they could end up losing it...
For the small businessman, often, at the end of the day,
the question he usually asks himself..."Is it really worth it?
Does it really matter? Do my patrons honestly care?"
Looking back...He truly tried to better his community.
Whatever he answers, life certainly was not boring...

I Lost A Friend Today...

I hadn't heard from Carmyn for a long time, therefore one Sunday night, a few weeks ago, I decided to phone her. She wasn't home, so I left a message stating that I'd love to hear how things were going and to give me a call. The next morning, her sister phoned me and told me that she had drowned that same week-end ...I couldn't believe it... I was totally stunned...

Carmyn and I had lost contact...to a certain degree. Every so often we'd call one another...talk about everything like we use to. My friend had been given a tough row to hoe...health wise...yet, she never complained...did what she had to do and lived each day as it came. I marvelled at her fortitude, her determination...If I wanted an example to use, it was right in front of me.

Carmyn met her love some years ago and married. He had children, she had children...yet, all seems to have worked out. I had never met her husband...only heard a lot of good attributes, therefore I was happy for her...she truly deserved this loving relationship.

As my friend, you helped me in so many ways...by your honesty and truthfulness...Thank-you...Good-bye, my friend...God Bless! I will miss you!!

Carmyn Grant died July 22, 2007.

I Lost A Friend Today...

"Hello! How are you today? Just passing through?"
" No, I'm new in town...Looking for something to do.
This neat little store has given me some clues.
Is your son Justin? My son's also in grade two."
"You have twin girls, Right?" I asked. "Quite a crew..."
"Hey! Bring your boys over to try some of my stew."
And I did...

At first...Carmyn was enigmatic...a puzzle...a mystery...
She was very discerning when revealing her story.
At times, I felt she was like an iceberg...10 percent
protruding...the rest hidden...inscrutable...a secret.
To feel safe, she'd disguise who she really was...
She talked little of past hurts...Those were her crosses...
She loved to listen...but, in what she would share...
very selective...For her to place trust was very rare.

In facing my weaknesses I learned compassion...
towards self and others...A win/win situation.
Not long after her arrival, my father passed-on.
In her eyes, men who showed their emotions
were honest...She cared not about impressions...
To her...real men expressed their love through passion...
And I proved her right...

People that you need will be brought to you...
What a beautiful affirmation...and so true.
Most people come merely for a short interlude,
yet, some leave me with much to brood...
then depart. Others become part of my life,
by their actions, feelings, and sometimes strife...
Often they leave too...but their spirit remains.
Carmyn was one of those...Now I feel pain...

Carmyn became a close friend...a confidant...
My marriage was on the rocks...I needed to rant...
Life was full of curves...I felt like a dissident,
somewhat of a rebel, whose cause was to vent...
She'd listen...ask questions...sometimes comment.
Today, I wonder if this was a reason she was sent.
I'll never know...

Going back...good memories flooded my mind.
It took her a long time to trust me...to unwind.
Finally, she felt comfortable in my surroundings...
When we got together, we talked about a lot of things...
To be honest...at times...we were like fire and ice...
To my moods and mood changes, she became quite wise.
She touched my life...by her words, by her conduct...
Her life-style was guided by providence, not by luck.

Carmyn wasn't trying to determine why she was here...
no...merely to understand. To do this she needed to peer
at options. Time to move on became very clear...
We'd shared many laughs over the past few years...
Now it was time to say good-bye...to shed a few tears...
Knowing it was right, she still had lots of fears...
My friend was gone...

How she saw life is how she tended to see herself ...
If she did as she ought...much personal wealth
was for the taking...without too much strife...
Yet, how she tended to see herself was how she saw life...
She wasn't looking for the world to entertain her...
yet, it did...on her schedule...without decoys or lures...
She understood her strengths, weaknesses and desires...
This gave her the choice to either conspire or inspire...

63

Sometimes in life we have to go away to come back...
What this means is a new path...a different track...
a change of attitude...A new love'll do just that...
For Carmyn, Tom's love was deep...He had the knack,
the ability of knowing when to give her some slack...
yet, also reassuring her that his love was intact.
This was Tom's beautiful gift ...

Wherever we go, we always take ourselves with us...
and on this road we are taught free-will and choices.
Sometimes Carmyn had great self-worth, which
was determined by her...yet, at times, there was a glitch...
To fix this, she'd talk to her heart for answers...
for this is where truth comes from...where it occurs...
She'd also talk to Tom for his view, his observation.
He'd point out a solution by explaining the problem...

Through words and actions...we are either the teacher
or the student. We discuss, we consult, we confer...
When she was a Social Worker she always wanted to stir
positive emotions and feelings...She became a seeker...
a searcher of truth...To succeed she could neither defer
nor deter...Looking back, many good things did occur...
Her role as parent being one...

Carmyn touched many lives on the path she chose...
yet, how many she affected...no one really knows.
At times she was so concerned...so full of worry...
Other times, she was a little girl, just full of glee,
so happy for others well being...She knew pain...
lots of pain...yet she never dwelled...she never blamed.
So strong emotionally...I admired her will power...
Today, only God knows why he made this her hour.

Her children were the winners...such a fine mom...
For them she had so much passion and compassion.
Looking back...they had always been the sum
of her life. She gave them wings...to become
self sufficient...to become their own person...
A total love, of which she would not succumb.
Quite a tribute to her kids...

Death happens one day... It doesn't happen in one day...
Thank God...He gives no clue of length of stay...
When our personal journey reaches it's end...
we'll be judged on our deeds...not our pretends...
I do believe your spirit will comfort your loved ones...
Your Creator will help you get this done...
if they ask...and, that's one of the stipulations...
To Ask...Humility is the key to this condition.

A friend is someone whom I've learned to appreciate...
someone I would use as example to emulate...
to try to be like...someone that's an advocate...
a support...Also, one who knows how to deliberate...
to reflect, to ponder. They will not criticize...berate...
By being around you, my world would illuminate
Carmyn...I lost a friend today...

To see their uncomprehending, forlorn expressions,
Carmyn's beautiful twins left me with the impression
of two young women adrift...unsure of their course...
They'd lost their best friend...their primary source.
They adored their mother...Never could they get enough.
The death of her body is not the death of their love...
Walking away from her interment, I felt a loss...
Carmyn's children were paying a hell of a cost.

Life Goes On When It's Over...

Another broken relationship has happened...and similar to all of those whom have passed this comparable route...they'll have to experience all the miseries, all the heart-aches, the second guessing, the denial, the anger, the fears...until, hopefully, they can either resolve their problems, usually through counselling, or they come to accept the inevitable...that it's over...and get on with their lives.

Why another poem of this sort? I thought the same question. My answer is...Although the end results are similar...and all the feelings are pretty much the same, the people involved are a unique couple...and this time there are health issues that are in play concerning the break-up. It may have played a big part in why it ended up the way it has. I sense, at times, this was a game, and sympathy was the main player...It worked for a while, but no more. Maybe I'm wrong, but that was my observation.

I'm not here to judge nor to give much advice...only to support. In whatever decision they reach, I'll try help them the best I can...which, in reality, isn't a great deal. Probably the best I can do is listen. It's important to let someone emotionally hurting, talk about it. I also have learnt from experience...life goes on when it's over...It just depends how quick or slow they want to get on with their lives.

Life Goes On When It's Over...

The note posted says you're leaving...That makes sense...
The way you've been acting...always on the defence...
We made the choices...we suffer the consequences...
together...I can see today, that's not your preference...
    Life...the stage show...an ever changing drama...
    Sounds like a little existentialism or perhaps karma...
    Your leaving has left me sensitively raw...

I've been waiting in time's ambush...knowing it would happen...
I guess some of my behaviour, I need not defend...
I realize you're tired...too many fences left to mend...
"I'm sorry" just doesn't cut it anymore...as an amend...
    I hate confrontations...arguments...as you well know...
    where you enjoy it. Sometimes you'd put on quite a show.
    I'm thinking you stuck around...merely to portray your halo...

Somewhere along our chosen path we went astray...
so, by choice, we each decided to go our own way,
to find the right direction...I realize we both strayed...
Bad decision emotionally...and, for that we paid...
    We knew no better, so our role models were our kin...
    instead of choosing our own game plan...We couldn't win.
    That was the start of the end, and we were just beginning...

In all honesty I knew you'd leave...wasn't sure when...
Life goes on when it's over...yet, I can't pretend...
In spite of everything, to me it feels like the end...
Like you, my mould, my model of life wouldn't bend.
    Love, it seems, has so many different sets of rules...
    at least for you...And to think, we had all the tools...
    I love you...No matter, the passion ran out of fuel...

Hope comes knocking on the door, and I answer;
"Go away...I'm soul searching ...and I can't defer..."
Not true...I was looking for a resolution to occur...
a band-aid solution...yet, one which you wouldn't deter...
    I feel a bit of guilt...thought I shouldn't...That's the past...
    And to think about worry is asinise...a bit crass...
    So, I use my old trick...ignore it...That's progress...

The thing that hurts...the kids were trying to make me see
that my life was so incongruous...truly an anomaly...
A good indicator has been my health difficulties...
and your callousness towards it...yet, you still blame me...
    What's my logic in trying to make you remember
    things you wanna forget? You too were a member
    of this dysfunctional arrangement...A true contender...

I had the chance to make my amends...yet I didn't...
Your actions displayed feelings that I shouldn't...
I felt you had no desire to hear...therefore you wouldn't
participate...Feeling like that, I guess you really couldn't...
    Yet, why do I sense you think you know my hand,
    when you leave impressions you don't understand...
    Maybe you've discovered what I wasn't saying...and ran...

Where are you heading?...I have no inkling, no clue...
To have no regrets, you gotta do what you gotta do.
We've had our difference...that's so very true,
yet...it's not all you...nor all me...It's me and you...
    I recall you telling me I'd always be a lonely man...
    until the day occurs when I come to like me...again...
    Thank-you for the tough love...Here's proof I can...

In all truth...I miss you...but, I know I have the power
within me to move on...I've reached that hour...
I must say...In our relationship you were the tower...
the strength...You really did try...and you never cowered.
    One thing that helped us, I believe, was our firm belief
    in our Creator...That never caused us any grief...
    and, today, that may be the key for turning a new leaf...

68

To Every Night There Is A Dawn.

The above picture was painted by artist <u>Jerry Doell.</u> This artist was having an exposition. When I saw the painting, I fell in love with it and bought it. I felt a real connection with this painting. A simple painting expressing so much spiritual meaning. The following poem are my feelings only.

69

To Every Night There Is A Dawn.

I awake with a start…hearing my little friend
frolicking in the dark…I try and pretend
that he's not there, for I desire more sleep…
No way! I see the moon's shadow trying to peep
into my small room…leaving it's many imprints
on it's way home from yet another long stint…
Groping around for my felt shoes and wool socks,
I find my wool pants and shirt…protection from the pox…

Most nights I'm glad I have my blanket of eider,
I once had a horse blanket…This is so much lighter…
and warmer…I pull the blanket over my head…
curl-up…and inhale the warmth of my enclosed breath.
My friend's movements remind me of my lot, my fate…
My role in life is solely to pray and meditate…
I love being a monk…talking to God through prayer…
asking Him in his gentleness and kindness to be fair…

I start to dress, feeling a bit of warmth through the vent
in my wall…An order of cloistered nuns are residents…
They do all the menial tasks…so their day begins
the same as us…They cook and we pray…for their sins…
and others…Smelling the gruel, my mouth salivates…
I hear sounds…I hurry for mass…It's a sin to be late…
I merely nod to my compatriots…We do not speak…
This is one of our vows…silence…God is all we seek…

After mass we eat porridge…then retreat to our rooms…
I feel so much comfort here…my sanctuary…my womb…
I virtually have nothing…yet, I believe I'm affluent
in God's world…His ways and mine are congruent…
Darkness has enveloped me…I just love this feeling…
this serenity…I know God is present…I feel his healing.
This is my time with Him…so, I get on my knees…
Starting my meditation with a prayer, I'm in no hurry…

I slowly get up…take a few paces to my papers…
which are sitting on my little oval table. It occurs
to me that I'm cold, so I light my wax candle…
for light and some heat…The holder's handle
and urn are terracotta…made of mud and earth…
The wax's design gives this useless vase some worth…
at least I think it does…Sitting down, I begin to debate…
Should I read, write my thoughts, or concentrate?

In the quiet of my mind, I glance around my room…
In one corner, the cot…in another…a few clothes strewn
about, beside my small dresser…then my petite table
and chair…and lastly, a little counter, which is capable
of holding a bowl, a pitcher and beside it a waste pail…
My crucifix…hangs over my bed…To the wall it is nailed…
What more materially do I need? Absolutely nothing…
I have clothes, food, shelter…and to God, my soul I bring.

I notice my worn, torn bible…and pick it up to read.
I truly believe every word written…This is my creed…
the symbol of my love for God…again and again.
Opening the good book, I hear the singing of a wren…
perched on my sill…I find a crumb in my pocket…
Opening my window, she's very happy to accept
my offer…and thanks me in verse, as she departs…
Her unconditional love brings singing to my heart.

Getting up, I peek outside my panel…to the skies above…
People who don't have dreams must find it very tough…
especially when looking up and seeing the wonders of God,
yet, denying His existence and presence when sought…
I can't see, nor touch Him…but I do feel His allure…
The peace and serenity I experience is the cure…
certainly at this moment…and that's all that matters…
Turning away…my thoughts I mull, discard, then gather…

It's still dark outside, yet the moon is full...
However, in short notice, I'll hear the gulls
screeching their presence, as daybreak soon begins...
I find my quill, my bottle of ink, and my string...
which, I twirl around my finger to concentrate.
How do I recognize a Higher Power? That's a debate
that'll continue till time stops...Reaching an inner peace...
with my conscience, my mind, my spirit...these are the keys...

Dipping my quill, I begin to write... *"How can I love you more?*
Do I understand all of your teachings...all your lore?"
I was taught...to be teachable, I need always to be humble...
"I've always tried to do right... though I've stumbled
from time to time...I was told the most powerful
way in making a decision was to reach into my soul...
stuff my pride...and ask You to make it for me...
This I have done...often...and it has set me free..."

Taking my bible, I go to The Beginning...'Genesis...'
Each day I have to continually remind myself of this...
How God created man to his image and likeness...
and continues to do so today...For that I am pious...
I notice my mother's pressed rose on the stones
at my feet...Her precious gift...for she had to loan
the shillings...She is so poor, yet so, so much love...
She taught me how to pray to our Lord up above...

Looking out my window, I see night has grown to dawn...
A new day, perhaps, but mine seems to be half gone...
The sun feels good...much warmth pouring through the pane...
Smoke arises from the extinguished candle's flame...
Near the candle holder, I place the rose on God's Book...
I go to my pitcher and bowl to wash...so I may look
presentable to my peers...as we gather for scripture...
Walking out my small door, I feel a slight flutter...

Running On Empty...

My friend has been running on empty for a long time, and we've talked about this dilemma, this predicament...She understands all the dynamics...the patterns, the changes, the variations and contrasts, yet she's having a hell of a time living all these dynamics...for most have been negative...and, many of them for a long time. She's experienced so many deaths in the past few months...Various concerning young and middle age people she knows. A few close family cousins...But the one that has really affected her was the accidental death of her brother whom she adored... This one, in particular, has taken a real toll on her physical and emotional well-being.

To add to these problems...her children...All are grown-up, on their own, yet there is always one of them back at home, trying to get out of one predicament or another, and using her goodness...which include her finances, her home, her food, her time...stuck doing all kinds of menial/time consuming tasks...Her work is also becomes affected... and her health is now in a precarious state, for she's not sleeping well, she's worried all the time...and the list goes on.

I could suggest to her to do or not to do so many things...but I won't. ...What I do suggest, though, is she continues living for today, that she ask her Creator for guidance, pray and meditate...Also, just maybe she could check out those feelings of anger and resentment...by doing an inventory on those subjects, and follow it up with feed-back from someone she trusts.
As you already know...the answers are there...Take care my friend.

Running On Empty...

Looking around my empty room...empty of all emotions...
I desire to be left alone...so I can go through the motions...
I am tired...physically, mentally and spiritually.
Lately, I've been wondering why I continue to dally...
wasting time, hanging around...I should just end it...
but, I can't...My Spirit is too strong to let me quit...

Have you ever felt being disliked for who you are?
What a feeling...especially when coming from family...
Those who wish I'd change, do so with an ardour...
because they are resentful... I do like the analogy...
Before criticizing...come...take a walk in my moccasins...
Perhaps, you'll catch a glimpse of where I've been...

Gazing across the field...the sun's pristine reflections
bounces off the snow...Unlike me...a faultless deflection...
I notice my fire is down to embers...I'm getting cold...
Pulling on a wrap, out the door I go...Wow! I feel old...
I need fresh air to clear the webs of my thoughts...
All around me, there's much anguish...things I never sought...

I know we have a lot of issues to resolve...
so, why aren't we attempting to find the solutions?
Why aren't we trying to really become involved?
No, It's simpler to mix a wee bit of collusion...
a little intrigue...so they may embellish our problems...
then, blame me for the outcome...It's easy to condemn...

Truth and lies...Truth and lies...Brushing the snow
off my old rocker, I sit in the sun's warm glow...
My mind wanders back to days of old...What a mess...
I recall, as a child, living near here ...lots of sadness...
My parents really tried ...life was hard...then, dad drowned...
Mom went to her family...She felt comfort in this surround...

74

Trying to imagine my kid's thoughts...I truly fail...
for, they're theirs...not mine...But, knowing me...
and, having traversed youth...my life was surreal.
How could it be conceivable for them to truly be
something other than what they are? Totally impossible...
Hence, for their actions, they don't feel accountable...

Extended family became security and truths...
They became my role-models in my youth.
The Creator was mentioned often and in reverence...
Also, our traditions were taught...These made sense...
though they got lost in time...because of my attitude...
I was trying things that altered my disposition, my moods...

It's not so much what I think...only my take on it...
An example: When thinking love...Am I thinking intimacy?
Maybe it's parents, or friends...Each a different fit...
When thinking about my children...my emotions get hazy...
I become muddled, confused...not because I don't love them...
No! Most times all I feel from them is feign and pretend...

On the Reserve, I had many siblings. This was home...
The family tried their best, but, I started to roam...
I grew tired of what was offered...I had things to do...
places to go, people who could give me what I was due...
I loved alcohol...I felt it gave me respect and courage...
Truth be known...it gave me false courage, and much rage...

In my culture, the woman wants to appease her children...
Is this wrong? Today, I certainly question this process...
Each time they make a wrong choice...again and again...
they invade my privacy...which causes me much stress...
"Let Go and Let God"..."Live and Let Live"...
I talk it, but don't walk it...I continue to give and give...

Walking to the wood pile, I gather a good armful...
The wood is like my thoughts...some needs to be culled.
Heading back to my cabin, my mind is really turning ...
If I could go back to where my thoughts are yearning...
in a flash I'd be there...Sadly, life won't let me dither...
I close my eyes and wonder why things are as they are?

I truly need someone...a friend, a counsellor...to confer...
Doubt slips into my thinking: Is change really possible?
This type of query sounds good, yet, I expect no answer...
for, it is a question that is nothing more than rhetorical...
I do feel, thought, that I really am running on empty...
My pain is deep, my sorrow is never relenting...

Throwing a few logs on the fire, I feel some heat...
I love solitude...I love my space and time...a treat...
I want to make some decisions...be it right or wrong...
My life's slipping by...I'm not ready for that final song...
not yet, anyways...Something I learnt from my mom...
To forgive others...first, start with myself...then move on...

There really needs to be changes so I can move ahead...
Certain beliefs and behaviours must be put to rest...
for this to happen...Somewhere I had once read:
'I can honour my children...and me...by giving up their quest...'
Let them research their morals, their philosophies...
Let them choose their paths...only then will we all be free...

Looking out my picture window, I notice some ptarmigans...
I wish I was like them...being able to meld, to blend
in their surroundings... I ask my Creator quite often...
to guide me, to show me the right way....Maybe I pretend...
thinking He is...but, the true test is telling me different...
I must be asking the wrong questions..."As a parent,
I have much repentance...Now, I need Your guiding hand...
In helping me attain some serenity...You choose the brand...and thanks"

Dreams Have No Expiry Date...

Psychologists say I dream every night. Who am I to dispute this, for most of my dreams I don't recall...yet, at times, there seems to be the odd one that sticks around, recurring fairly often. These, if I continue to dream them, and I also continue to remember them, I try and break them down to see what the root cause of the dream is, and what can be done to stop it from returning...if anything. Usually what happens is after a period of time, the mind decides to store them away...as if to say..."that was fun, but now it's time for you to worry about other trivial issues...I might bring them back in the future...just to see if you'll react differently..."

It really is amazing how my mind can recall so many incidents in my lifetime. Like a recorder, my mind has a fast-forward, pause, rewind, seek, and stop...and while I'm in my REM sleep, this is when dreaming occurs. Dreams, often, are reconstruction of issues happening in my life at the stage that I'm at...Money problems, kids, marital, or perhaps erotic desire...yet, that's not necessarily true...images change constantly, going back and forth from years gone by to today, and people also change...from setting to setting. How and why they are there is beyond me...yet they are.

Many of the dreams that I recall, I wish they would disappear forever, but of the good feeling dreams that I remember, I wish they'd stick around forever...One thing I do know...good or bad...dreams have no expiry date.

Dreams Have No Expiry Date.

I wonder what it's like being rich...
In my dream, I'm giving myself a pinch...
yet, looking behind me...There has to be a hitch.
It's hard to imagine crossing that bridge...
it really is...I seem to lack the courage,
even though, for some it seems to be a cinch.
>If only dreams were true... I love my fate...
>I hope I never wake. This is too great.
>Thank God!...Dreams have no expiry date...

Imagine! Understanding my own kids actions?
I must be dreaming! I usually have a reaction...
often belittling their conduct...a detraction...
Of course, this gives them so much satisfaction,
much delight...even if it's for a small fraction
of time...Knowing my anger, they make traction.
>Sometimes I picture that we can relate...
>In my dream, their feelings I contemplate,
>and, rightly ponder them...to praise, not berate.

In my dream...sweet Alexis is my princess...
an appealing little lady without any duress.
A big happy nectarous smile...so infectious...
making my heart quiver...I must confess.
I just want to touch her skin...to caress...
She is so beautiful...I was truly blessed.
>Seeing her with her dolls, wanting them to emulate
>her feelings, her young wondrous mind creates
>different settings... making it easier to facilitate.

78

Who is that loud mouth trying to intrude?
I don't recognize the face, nor the brood...
Wait a minute! That's that famous hockey dude...
He's coming over...I'd heard he's a real prude...
Tagging along is some broad who's pretty rude...
I wonder why they're in my dream? She's so crude...
      For some unknown reason, I seem very frustrated...
      I hope he doesn't think I'm going to mediate...
      This is weird...Ah well! I'll give it to him straight...

Where did all my loves go over the years?
Turning around...they've all seem to disappear...
I was good at pretending, making things appear
wholly different than truth...Blame was always near.
Looking back...I lost...mostly through fear...
I was so afraid to look at my soul...my mirror.
      In my images...most past loves I indeed ache...
      yet, often, shadows emerge...willing to wait.
      Thank God; Dreams have no expiry date.

I dream of many personal issues, of which
I have no control, yet they make me flinch.
That's when I ask my Creator to bridge
this gap...by helping me understand the glitches.
He shows me what to keep, what to switch...
It becomes simple...like eating oatmeal porridge...
      In most of my pictures... Time alleviates
      the pain, the sorrow. My mind certainly aids
      this by being honest, and not prevaricate.

Sometimes I dream I'm at some celebration ...
wondering why I'm there...certainly an aberration.
Some people are old, some are new creation,
some I don't recognize, others are relations.
All are jovial, at least in the dream's duration ...
Why I was there...I have no inspiration.
   Was I invited as part of the congregate?
   I don't know...my dream suddenly dissipates,
   leaving me with a taste of sour grapes.

Hi Mom! Hi Dad! Hi Claire! Nice seeing you.
Observing all three ...What's the occurrence...what's new?
You seem sad...Is there something I didn't construe,
I didn't quite understand? Often I don't have a clue
on what's happening...or on what I'm to do...
I feel your loving aura...helping me stay true..
   This apparition seems weird, yet I appreciate
   your concern...I'm fortunate...you can anticipate...
   I miss you immensely...Thanks for keeping me straight.

As morning approaches and I finally wake,
I twinge...My head has a slight ache.
That's a symbol, indicating I did partake
in a lot of dreams...Many scenes I did create...
One, I slightly recall...I was grilling steak,
savoring the smell...beside a beautiful lake.
   Ah! Good memories...They illuminate
   my whole. To keep them intact...I animate...
   I encourage my mind to fully participate.
   Thank God; Dreams have no expiry date.

Full Of Wonder...

Most of my poems have been quite serious lately...and I guess it was my choice in the reasons why I wrote them...I felt it was now time to put a bit of humour in my writing...so I did.

In this poem, this old gent is explaining his grievances, because he's getting on in life...Unfortunately time doesn't go back...as this man starts to grasp, by wondering where the time went to. He realizes he now has a lot of legitimate reasons for grumbling. It doesn't seem so long ago that he was a productive, fairly happy type...and really it wasn't...Yet here he is today, starting to get a touch of dementia...and not pleased with that.

Enjoy!

Full Of Wonder...

I awake yelling "shut-up," trying to find the button
to silence that darn alarm...Reaching for my glasses,
they fall on the rug..."Can you help me out here hon?
I'm blind as a bat..." Moments of years gone by, flashes
through my brain...the time I crushed them all to pieces...
by stepping on them...You'd a thought it was world's end...
by the way dad spoke...He sure did use the name of Jesus...
Being young, I thought they were pretty good friends.

> I kinda wonder where those years have gone to...
> I mean, time is passing by...To where? I've no clue...
> There was a time, I thought, I'd have lots of fame...
> and certain that folks would know me by my name...
> Of course it never happened...a fantasy...a pipe dream,
> led by my ego...I guess age has made me a bit serene...
> though, not sure what it means...Ah well! C'est la vie...
> At my age, I don't have to know it all...or even agree...

The ole babe, she found them for me...Putting them on...
Eureka! Now, what was I gonna do before they got lost?
Ah well, it don't matter...as I slowly head for the john...
Looking out the window, I see the panes full of frost.
Hearing the radio, I wondered if I had shut it off...
I'm positive I did...even though I don't remember...
I wonder if I'd taken my medicine for my cough...
So, smacking my lips, I use the saliva as my lure...

> I kinda wonder what the future still holds for me...
> I mean, it seems all I do, all day long, is pee...
> and my hearing...well forget it...It's gone to pot...
> Maybe I should try that...Probably get caught...
> At least I'd have something good to say on my tomb...
> Trying to remember what I'd forgotten, consumes
> my waking hours...which aren't too many anymore...
> If I ain't sleeping, I'm peeing...My daily chores...

Interested in local gossip, I switch on the cable...
Turning the corner, I notice the business page,
so, I pick it up and head for the breakfast table.
The news is explaining how this entrepreneur is so sage...
in the billions he's gained...by cheating his customers...
Whoopie Ding! It sure smells like a crock of B.S...
but, I sure do like that smell of coffee...Yes Sir!
Taking a sip, I spill it everywhere...My what a mess...

      I kinda wonder what's gonna happen in this very day...
      to hell with tomorrow...Yet, I know my mind will stray
      back into my past and forward into the future...
      Hey...That's where I came from...that what I remember...
      and, it's where I'm going...something I don't wanna miss...
      Therefore, I'll leave today to become someone else's gist,
      while I prepare for tomorrow...Makes sense to me...
      and really...I could care less if anyone else agrees...

Jees, there's a lot of noise...I can't even think straight...
The radio, the TV, the old lady yappin' about nothing...
I wish they'd all shut-up...How can I concentrate?
Oh my God! Now that stupid, useless phone is ringing...
I answer...It's my brother-in-law wanting to go for a beer...
I said no! He'll want me to sit in that stink hole all day...
watch him get drunk...What a loser...Nobody wants to hear
his crap...He'll forget his way home again, then he'll stray...

      I kinda wonder how much more time I have left...
      At one time, I was very handy...quite deft...
      not anymore...Struggling through the day is tough enough...
      I complain about the ole gal...but, she's the one I love.
      I'm starting to feel some fear...I ain't never been religious...
      I know nothing about this God, but I do know how to cuss...

I'm kinda wondering...if I learn a prayer or two...
if there's really a chance...so that I may continue
on this rocky road to who knows where...maybe Galilee...
Ah! Forget it...I'm tired, I'm grouchy, and I need to pee...
Sleep, my friend, come to me...You're my saviour...
Can't remember if I took my medicine...so I swore...

The Spirits From The Past...What Would They Say?

One of the courses I took, some years back, was on Native Issues. It was a real eye opener. I held a certain amount of the stereo typing of my own about our Aboriginals, yet, by being around them all of my childhood... we lived in North Battleford, Saskatchewan, which has many Reserves surrounding it...I did have some empathy, some compassion. What this course introduced me to was the misconceptions directed towards these people. Many people blame the native for the problems they are having... They feel they are lazy...living off welfare, taking advantage of the white man's generosity, plus, of course, being a bunch of drunks. They should work instead of filling up the jails, and living off our kindness...

To go back in history, the many Nations have such rich cultures, such an interesting story. I'm sure they didn't want to lose that and felt to keep this heritage, this tradition, they would need to come to an understanding and agreement with the white government...so they finally agreed to come to the table to discuss and accept the terms presented. This became known as The Indian Act, and that was what all parties signed. In essence, the Aboriginals were guaranteed land, healthcare, education, and food...These Rights are still in existence and are still a guarantee today...if people live on the Reserves...Also, those that live off the reserves, yet have a treaty number...are granted certain privileges and concessions.

I tried to express in this poem some of the issues facing the Native today. It is merely a glimpse...for there is so much I have no knowledge of, or to present it would take many pages. One thing I do know from all the research I did...for I wrote a term paper on this very issue...is The Canadian Government has been, and I suspect are still trying to assimilate the native culture...How would you like your language, your customs, your beliefs, your values...all the things you were taught...to be taken away from you, and then forced you to learn a whole new set of rules, which are alien to your philosophy, impressing on you a whole new set of values and beliefs. I suspect not too many of us would be willing to do that...yet, we expect the Aboriginals to comply...without complaints.

I wonder what the spirits of the past would think and say about the way their people are treated today...An interesting thought!

The Spirits From The Past...What Would They Say?

Traditions: Language, dress, mannerism ...our culture...
This is what should guide us and give us pleasure.
Our language expresses how we are attached to nature...
Our dress and food does the same...We were nurtured...
by berries, by herbs, by wild game to exist...to endure...
Our spirits are also entwined in this procedure...
The eagle, the owl, the wolf...these represent rapture...
and pain...If on a quest...many things can and do occur.

In trying to understand my culture, what do I see?
Customary beliefs and social form that don't agree.
We believe in the elders...their rulings, their decree...
Their role is wisdom and truth...not lies and deceit...
Our tradition of lodges and purging...is a healthy fee,
as is the chanting and drum dances...to help set us free.
Another belief...our hunting rights, we won't concede...
To all of this our belief in The Creator...That's the key...

We were granted land, education, food, and healthcare...
and, we were primed to feel lucky for them being so fair...
But in truth, we were made very much aware,
that we were the chattels of Government Affairs.
We were stuck in remote locations, and doled-out welfare...
Our dignity, our self-respect was in total disrepair...
Our pride came out of a bottle of whiskey...Our lair
was claptrap shacks and tents...which many had to share...

Yet, on the other side of the coin is the social unrest...
In many ways we are under so much social duress...
Our culture is very rich...Why seek others style of dress?
And we do...because of insecurities...causing such a mess!!
Many turn to alcohol and drugs...These we need to wrest...
so we may curb abuse...This sickness leaves many to digress
What they crave is love...To be held...To be caressed...
Instead, the anguish leads to suicide...They're so depressed...

85

Education is suppose to be knowledge...the main source
of learning...the ability to teach...A chance to discourse...
The white man, in all his wisdom, wanted to follow this course...
so...Residential Schools, in far away places...was enforced,
to assimilate our culture...Then forcing us to endorse
their customs...They attained their goal. To fulfill their purpose...
they sexually and emotionally abused children...by force...
For many still today, these humiliating horrors still distorts
the mind...No words could describe any type of remorse...

When looking at material security...we're impoverished...
The Indian Act...for us...has very little accomplished...
We're put on reservations, causing much anguish...
Our style of education merely helps the vices flourish...
for, the classes are the streets...Many feel they're envious...
They have this drug money, which becomes a real fetish...
In playing this type of game, many die...Another cherished
loved one to mourn...So senseless...Absolutely hellish...

Upon relinquishing our ways, we were guaranteed
health and nourishment. This was also part of the treaty...
No one had transportation...Our chiefs had to plead
for some sort of rudimentary services...Finally, it was agreed
that some aid...not much...but some, would be a certainty...
In the end, most felt more comfortable with the berries,
herbs, and spices of the Medicine Man...His word, none heeded...
for nature had always provided...They respected his creed...

It's no wonder we want our own sovereignty...
All we've been promised are simply ambiguities...
or outright lies...We can't live with uncertainties...
Perhaps self governing is the answer to all incongruities...
We could help young girls cut back on pregnancies...
by building self-esteem...or teach about the trees...
about nature...to our young men...Also, about anonymity...
to become content with self...the foundation of humility...
Am I dreaming? I hope not...We need not more anomalies...

The Indian Agent was appointed to the band, to supervise...
and, to be it's purveyor...In all honesty, some were wise...
For most, though, this power, was too much of a prize,
and they took advantage through schemes they devised...
The Sundance's and Pot Latch banquets were criticized
for creating turmoil and unrest...and banned through lies...
When bands took control...they had no idea, nor realized
the havoc, the devastation these agents had contrived...

Observing our life-style today, I have much fear...
Many of our leaders are an enigma...Akin to a mirror,
they reflect honour...yet, dishonour is what appears...
Many issues and concerns...they have no desire to hear...
Our traditions...our beliefs, which include a seer,
are becoming less important...Our new Manitou is clear...
Casinos, gambling, alcohol...These are our new peers...
This is the evil spirit's work, causing many tears...

Many of our people have been degraded for so long...
It really isn't any wonder that we feel we don't belong...
By the colour of our skin, how can we be judged felon?
But we are...and often...Most feel inferior, not strong...
Our elders had taught us we were all equal in opinions...
and in opportunity...Not true! Amongst the throng,
we're not wanted...Why do we continue to prolong
the inevitable...Many are starting to combat this wrong...

Glimpsing and reflecting on our recent dismal history...
The spirits from the past...What would they say?
I suspect they would feel a lot of shame, today...
I believe they would be saddened by all the vices in play...
Booze, Drugs, Prostitution...What a catastrophe...
often ending with jail...or worse...suicide...A sad story...
I can hear them...insisting on The Creator to show the way...
The lodges and sweet grass...Traditions...Not apathy...

Making An Impression.

Who in life won't leave some sort of impression? I believe everyone will. Some people, well they'll leave very good impressions, while others will tend to leave bad impressions. If, by chance, you come to know a person quite well, then he/she will probably leave you with many impressions...and over time you will come to accept their reputation as well as understand some of the of the traits that make up their character ...through these impressions that you gathered.

But, by chance, if you encounter a person only once or twice...then first impressions are usually the ones we remember ...good or bad. Males more so than females, often like to impress through the use of language...be it articulate, be it slang, be it the expressions of the era...whatever.

This poem is about trying to impress....A lot of people, especially men, will be able to identify with the character in the poem. I did meet someone like this a long time ago, and for a little while this fellow was placed into my life. At first I thought he was so cool, so right-on. It didn't take very long to change directions concerning the impressions he was leaving me with. I changed towns and haven't seen him since...thought after all these years, I still can picture the impressions he left me with...and most are quite negative.

Making An Impression.

Man, I feel so incredibly important.
People are just in awe of my terminology.
I can't remember when I became so efficient...
It must be my mental state, my psychology.
I just love showing folks my true colours...
It makes me feel superior, so much taller.

Everybody wants to portray my style,
I'm sure. I mean, it depicts such class...
even if I haven't washed in a while...
or that my shirt and jeans 're trash...
and...contrary to many beliefs...countless
are joining...They, too, want to impress.

Getting into a chat with these recruits
is very enlightening, to say the least.
Some, with their shifty eyes, appear shrewd...
missing nothing...Similar to a grand feast,
they have so much to offer... eloquence
un-matched... revealing no pretence.

The climate has altered ever so slight.
Like the weather, I perceive some modifications...
Some are saying that... maybe I'm not right...
maybe I should have more consideration
of others opinions and their feelings.
Not today...Life's about wheelin' and dealin'.

Thinking it over, perhaps I don't know
the language as well as I first thought.
All my friends made me feel like a hero...
I was so smart; I didn't need to be taught.
Not true. I know I'm very quick, albeit
I realize my language is more for the night.

Duplicating every second word seems bizarre.
Actually people look at me kinda strange…
Maybe my brilliance is like the North Star…
very noticeable, but way out of range,
and, that's okay… I'm making an impression.
Possibly some will learn from this lesson.

I sense some people don't want much to do
with my type. They are labelling me a radical…
whatever that means…I don't have a clue…
For them, it's important to name call…
I guess…We only speak about women,
God, kids, and our special rights as men.

Some of my so-called 'friends' are asking
me when I'll be changing some of my antics.
I don't know why they want me to be masking
some of my behaviour…It's no pandemic,
and, it's sure not endemic…widespread…
Why do I discern some are feeling a dread?

I'm kinda wondering how this all happened…
I've acquired the reputation of notoriety.
People have no couth, always making me defend
my words, my actions…plus my deity…
Who cares if I don't believe in God…No big deal…
Anyways, I do have one moral…I don't steal…

Who hasn't used God's name in vain?
Which man claims not to have said salacious
things about women's anatomy and brain…
or kids and their mothers who are so frivolous?
Hey! I'm not a judge…but, I do like swearing…
It's my rights as a man, which I enjoy sharing.

If It Ain't The Darkest Hour...It's Pretty Close...

Some time ago I met this lovely young woman, thought she never felt like that. She'd moved because she and her husband were split-up. She had family to come to, and it felt like the best thing to do... My friend was running from her past, yet living fully in it...What a contradiction...and that's exactly what it was... wanting love, respect, and acceptance, yet taking what came along because she had none of this inside of her. You can only give away what you possess.

A few short months ago, she cried out for help...Someone was there to guide her down a different path than the one she'd been on. In no time, this gal had changed her life-style quite drastically. Supposedly everyone was happy to see the changes...Not true...There were some close to her who wanted her to change...as long as they continued to dictate her life... Impossible! Either you're on board or you're not.

That's where this poem comes from... Confrontation with love... explaining what needs to be changed, so that everyone is on the same page. For most people that is so difficult to do...they would rather leave things be, than stir the pot and right the issues that are wrong. But, she did it, in spite of it being very difficult. I'm sure she was probably saying: "If it ain't the darkest hour...it's pretty close..." In making this decision she had two questions to ask herself: 1) Was it right for her? 2) Did it harm the other person? The first answer was yes, the second answer was no...Bravo!

If It Ain't The Darkest Hour...It's Pretty Close...

The heaviness in my heart spells pain...
and does it ever hurt...a real strain.
I'm so fearful to expose what it contains...
yet, I don't understand why...It's my gain.
I question why I'm thinking of past ghosts...
If it ain't the darkest hour...it's pretty close.

I certainly was not a leader...but I was a disciple
of a 'Dark Force'. He taught me his principles.
He cared not about my weakness or my strengths...
No, he taught me his instincts...A reminder of what hell
was all about...on earth...I was caught in his spell...
and because of it I practiced many different pranks.
Because of my life-style, I've never had many successes...
mostly failures...so this is rather new...lots of guesses,
and that scares me. The old habits were so comfortable...
I knew what to expect, though not many were reliable.

My up-bringing took away my pride, my self-esteem.
I felt others were always judging me...or so it seems,
but truth be known, it was I who was judging self.
I need to bring, not only receive...to fulfill my dream...
my dream of loving me...to understand what that means.
Because of worry and fear, I question my choices...
No confidence, and that is wrong...If my inner voice
agrees to my selection, plus I do not harm another...
maybe a bruised ego...my choices I need to hover.

In spite of the shame those memory reels do bring.
In thinking about it, I realize that guilt hurts me...
no one else. Change is so frightening...I want to cling
to that known past...to continue having the odd fling...
but, then I feel guilty again...I just wanna flee.
>If I went back to my past ways of no commitment,
>I know for sure that Child Welfare would be sent...
>Despite all my bad choices, I still mined a few gems...
>My kids are all I really got, and now I'd lose them.

Feeling all these old fears...and new ones too...
I start to wonder if it could be actually true...
those stories about old qualms that never quite die.
Why is it they slink off and hide like a shrew
in some corner...waiting for that occasion anew...
than making their appearance ever so, so sly.
>It seems life got in the way of my plans...
>even if I didn't have any, for I always ran...
>from honesty, wisdom, and truth...from me...
>not taking responsibilities gave me consent to flee.

Looking at the other side of this equation,
I felt some used me...through their justifications...
Talk about getting angry...What right did they possess
to emotionally rape me? Total exploitation...
I felt indignant...yet, didn't demand an explanation,
for, it mattered not...My friend, fear, made me regress.
>I can't go on letting people walk all over me,
>especially those so near. If I continue to let worry
>and fear rule...I give others the power of control...
>over me, my kids...my life. Good-bye to my soul

All things that happen in my life are like a dance...
trying to figure out the steps, the movements...the balance...
In picturing who I am, this reflects where I belong...
If I look at destiny...my fate, my fortune...then decisions
are needed. In this assessment I'm able to make incisions...
slotting my pleasures or displeasures...Is this so wrong?
        They tell me I am responsible for my success...
        I'm not so sure...I tend to screw-up and leave a mess...
        I wish I had more confidence...more self-worth...
        Actually, I wish I was that child learning to have mirth...

As I ponder on what I need to change, to alter,
I ask: " Is the life I'm leading enough, or does it matter?
Or, perhaps this same life doesn't want to live in me..."
I'm starting to learn...slowly...that I do have some power...
to get beyond this fear and conquer something better.
In doing so, I need to learn acceptance...that's the key.
        I know that I'm worried sick...my hands are shaking.
        Thinking about it has my heart-beat palpitating.
        Phew! How do I go about this...this approach...
        In the old days I'da got out my clip and roach...

        Today I talked to the person causing me so much fear.
        I was very scared...my eyes were brimming with tears...
        It took all of my strength to make myself clear...
        for she was in total denial...she didn't want to hear.
        By her words, I visualized appearances of past ghosts...
        Thinking about it...a beer was what I wanted the most...
        but, help was what I asked for instead...Who knows?
        If this ain't the darkest hour...it's very, very close...

Silence And Solitude.

The setting for this poem comes from an old trapper's cabin in the Rocky Mountains, between Golden and Radium Hot Springs in B.C. I had gone there on four different occasions, and having spent the whole day and night on three of the four times, I felt quite comfortable in this surroundings. This cabin had a small lake in front, and mountains and forest surrounding it. There were trails to discover, plus, you had to walk approximately a ½ a mile to get to the cabin.

I loved it out there...I based this poem on this setting...yet, the many issues that happened in my life after I moved away from there is what I'm writing about in this poem...I used this mountain scene as my physical background...Over time, and through silence and solitude I've learnt how to deal with many emotional issues that have presented themselves over the years.

Today, I've learnt to take my space and time for myself...I need my solitude...my silence...so that I can deal with "The Real World." I often think of that old cabin...what great memories...

Silence And Solitude

Having made the decision to take a few days off...
I chose for my retreat, a solitary hunters cabin...
nestled in the Rockies...with a little lake in front...
I love the outdoors, even though I don't hunt...
I love the solitude...For me it's an overall win/win...
Giving me time to soul search...to dig out my stuff...
Tranquility and harmony...sets the tone
for my solitude...letting me feel right at home...

The air feels crisp, smarting, yet I love it...
It's a good wake-up call, giving me a chance
to understand some of my emotions, my feelings,
during my solitary walk...Perhaps some healing
may occur...something I thrive for...But, at a glance
I'm not sure...I hope so...I do know I won't quit...
I've been taught You often answer in silence...
yet, I wonder if I'm capable to truly sense...

Where I come from, they would call this lake a pond...
yet, sitting and fed by mountain streams...so pristine...
unspoiled...this lake and setting leave me in awe...
Sitting on a stump, I marvel at the beauty...and flaws...
The precariously balanced trees...so fragile...so lean...
their exposed roots in the crevices...and beyond...
I often feel like those trees, that's for sure...
but, at this moment, I feel at peace with nature ...

Getting up, I hear the hums of silence...The birds chirping,
the breeze's soft rustling, the creek subtly gurgling...
I feel completely engulfed within this sound's rhapsody...
This silence invites me to question my life today...
Tasting a few of my issues...some seem to be curdling...
The samples tell me there are things to the table I must bring...
What do I hear in the silence of my mind?
Let go and let God...it's time to unwind...

Walking back to the cabin, I notice how decrepit
this old shelter has become...I have much empathy...
Loneliness articulates the pain of being alone...
of no one caring...The old structure creaks and groans
from lack of care...If it had a soul, I'm sure it would say,
"I've seen a lot...I have much to say...Come and sit..."
The rewards that come only in the moments of solitude...
I enjoy them... for they are mine to translate, to construe...

Sitting on the crippled precarious chair, I feel embraced...
totally immersed in silence...the glory of being alone...
Not long ago, feelings like these wouldn't have happened...
Fear wouldn't have let it transpire...Today, I use my pen
to transcribe these doubts...then figure out my zones...
my morals...my values, my beliefs...issues I need to face...
Actually, the sanctuary, the shelter solitude offers,
comes from within...this is my treasure, my coffer...

Getting up, I wander into this one room crooked shack...
I love it! The feel of age, of wisdom permeates these walls...
I light a fire in the old wood stove...for it is damp...
Gathering my pack, I find my little pocket lamp...
It's getting dark...and my hungry stomach growls...
Finding a pot, beans are my feast...Soon I hit the sack...
Silence is a communion...a unity with nature...
Something I want to participate in...and to nurture...

I don't recall dreaming, for I had hardly moved...
but, before falling asleep, I noted the pine smell,
and the cool mountain air. I slept like a baby...
For the first time in a long, long time I feel free...
What a feeling! This location has me in a spell...
I feel a change of attitude...a new life-style groove...
Does it matter where a man had been...or what he's done?
No! It's what he feels within...His road to the sun.

97

Stepping out onto the small porch…I look up…
The mountain stares me in the face…What a sight!
The water…a soft blue…portraying snow-capped peaks…
reflections off the perfect mirror… something nature concedes…
allowing me to marvel at the beauty…It's such a delight…
something I want to relish…to fill my soul…to fill my cup…
          Allowing myself to experience this exquisiteness…
          I observe another side of nature…it's daintiness…

I feel a sadness, for I know I must leave soon…
but not just yet…Finding my old stump, I sit…
I notice the fish are feasting on the many flies…
by the creases in the water…Something nature supplies…
It amazes me how the landscape is so tightly knit…
like a puzzle…everything fits perfectly…not strewn…
          This delicacy of nature is beyond compare…
          Thank God, man had no say in this creation so rare…

Getting up…I stand in the silence and truly listen…
for, this was God's first language…silence…
and mine today…to discover my candour, my truths…
In my past I coped with issues by being aloof…
Not today…Honesty has removed this pretence…
Some faults are exposed…and, now a few amends…
          Silence gives me a chance to meditate with my Creator…
          where humility teaches me to quit being a debater…

It's time to go…everyday life has started to intrude…
As I'm packing my few articles, to God I confer…
thanking Him for showing me solitude is a one to one…
          Everyone has a story…and it should be told…everyone…
          though many feel they really have nothing to offer…
          This type, I know, would feel comfort in solitude…
When a dream dies…often we feel stripped…denuded…
Don't be afraid to place humility before ego…for sure…
just by wanting…your answers have already begun…

          Prayer and meditation in silence and solitude…

Hate...The Power Of An Evil Spirit...

As I was growing up, I was taught that Life meant a great deal, and I was taught to respect mine and others...I've never forgotten this...I have always tried to treat others with respect. I can also say, it didn't always work...In fact, there were times my thoughts were not nice...and, even if the expression, "taking a life" was in my lexicon, it was beyond me to fulfill this type of action.

Today, when I read or hear about the chaos and senseless killings in Afghanistan, Iraq, Pakistan, Lebanon, Iran, Israel...and the many more Countries...I shudder. All the killings...the destruction...Life means absolutely nothing...I get the feeling, because of repetition, because of continuous media coverage, that we are becoming so desensitized, so callous to these events...and that is exactly what these evil spirits want us to feel

I've experienced death...as have most people. When a person you love dies, there is a certain amount of grief...depending on age, on sickness, on suffering. Sometimes, even though we will miss the loved one, we are glad their suffering is over. When it comes to children...the pain is usually quite intense...so painful...

When it comes to killings and death caused by these car bomber, or dictators trying to wipe out a whole sect...as examples...the pain, the grief, the hatred caused cannot be described, yet the pain felt by so many, causes retributions...and the cycles continue..."An eye for an eye..." This makes God's nemesis...God's arch-rival revel in celebration.

I'm not sure what the answer is...but it isn't what's happening today. I would not be afraid to wager that love and forgiveness would solve many of these problems...or perhaps a little compassion and kindness, or perhaps a little humility instead of control by our ego...Actually, there are a lot of things that could change...positive changes...Something to think about.

Hate...The Power Of An Evil Spirit...

In words and action...you're judged by where you come from...
unfortunately...Many, many folk live off mere crumbs
for their existence...and are judged as bums and/or dumb...
When opinion of self is contempt...then self we malign...
Then, evil powers unleashes the ego...hoping to blind...
This power...this energy...plays games with their minds...
This is exactly what these evil spirits are counting on...
Hateful emotions...feelings that they are treated wrong...
and need to get revenge... Odium becomes the song...

Upon digging a little deeper into my feelings...in conjunction
to world happenings...my thoughts are in a fluctuation ...
I don't quite understand all the strife...all the dissention...
Newspapers and TV leave me mostly with a bad taste...
To feel the hate projected because of colour, creed or race,
is mind numbing...Life means nothing...such a waste!!
mostly because of religion...That's not God's Way...
True enough...religion is based on spirituality...
yet, spirituality requires no religion to convey...

Outwardly...the world is a mess...It makes me question...
when I see human rights condemned...causing so much tension...
Whoever's in charge is surely teaching the wrong lessons...
Then I realise who the educators are: Cheaters and stealers...
cloaked as spiritual leaders...pretending to be teachers...
They're the masters at deceiving...gathering parasites and leeches...
The hatred they portray as just and proper...is all poison...
true malice...That's the power of this fiend...this demon...
They induce, then seduce you in thinking they can do no wrong...

In keeping the population ignorant…that is the ace card
of any extremist group…That way it isn't too hard
to give people choices…either follow…or die by the sword…
I know I'm not the sharpest knife in the drawer…
but…even I can see what humans can do with power…
They portray their righteousness…by calling on the cowards
to prove their validity…Many together, entice much fear…
Killing and maiming…total destruction…causing many tears…
The results? Vengeance! There are no changes in the mirror…
The cycle continues…All of a sudden we all become seers…

Hate…the power of an evil spirit…the devil in disguise…
Smoke and mirrors… illusive and fallacious…all lies…
This is happening right here right now…The devil is wise…
He dangles affluence to a capitalist…Riches is the key…
To those who are starving, he brings them to their knees
through starvation, then promises them food…for a fee…
They must promise him total control…No ands, ifs or buts…
To the religious fanatic…he gives them free rein to strut
to embrace their hate-filled beliefs…and calling it just…

Even though from time to time they may need some repairs…
some adjustments…my values, for me, are easy to wear…
Mulling through my thoughts and feelings…I do care…
I do care for my morals, my beliefs…Somewhat of an altruist…
I do believe in God, and I have trouble understanding atheists…
Also, Islam and jihad…and their holy war…It's a big cyst…
War is war…and, it's not holy… at least I don't think so…
In planting hate, will holy and love be what we sow?
I want love not hate…and not just rhetoric…I want show…

God must just shake His head…By having given man choices…
So many choose evil in their poise…and in their voice…
I'm sure God understands why many are killed or destroyed…

But, I don't…I guess that's why I'm not God…THANK GOD!!

101

I Asked God For A Friend...He Presented You...

Actually, for a number of years I decided to live a single life. I've often thought about getting into a relationship...but when I'd analyse my emotional costs, let alone everything else, I'd always decide to continue on the road I was on...It felt comfortable and no hassles...

But, ideas change, life-style change...One day I experienced a feeling that it was time to try something different...maybe meet-up with a woman ...see what would happen. I was willing to give it a shot...and voila, not long after that I met Kathy.

I knew her from past encounters. She was always friendly, and I enjoyed her warm smile...but, in all honesty we were merely acquaintances. How and why we met is another story...

Kathy...Thank-you! As the title states, I asked God for a friend, and He presented you...Without a doubt, I am the fortunate one...Thanks for your love...I love you a lot.

I Asked God For A Friend...He Presented You...

I enjoy being alone...In fact, there were many times
I thrived on it...My decisions...and no one to whine...
Some told me I was losing out on many good things...
Not sure what...This was a lot better than what I had...
I never enjoyed mind games...I would get so mad...
which, caused guilt and remorse...my emotional sling...

For years I felt I had no right to bring another
into my life...My kids could have used a mother...
and hindsight indicates that...without a doubt...
Was it stupidity, stubbornness, ego or pride?
Not sure! Whatever...this was my single ride...
my problems...no one else's...and I chose the route.

After my sons left home I caressed sadness...and relief...
Sadness...because I felt, in many ways, like a thief...
I'd not done a worthy job in raising my boys...
yet, I've come to understand that the skills I had
was all I knew...lessons I had been taught as a lad...
The relief? Our bond, thought fractured, was not destroyed.

The empty nest felt good...and it still feels good...
Knowing what I know today, I'm positive I would
use an altered approach...if I had a second chance...
The resentments I'd harboured was my main demise...
and, the kids I often blamed ...through different disguises...
By putting on discrete masks...I could justify my annoyance.

I have had some opportunities to get involved...
but...I chose not to...My life's puzzle was not resolved...
I was missing a few pieces, which had to be found.
When I stopped living in the problem, I was granted a key...
It showed me how to live in the solution...and abate worry...
Life only becomes a riddle if I let issues compound...

Through self-analysis...if I wished a worthwhile
meaningful life...then I needed to adjust my life-style...
completely...I've been given a chance to realize...
that in spite of my alcoholism...I could change...
I discovered many issues I needed to rearrange...
and to gain success...to many I needed to apologize...

In many ways, life is like a play...I've learnt to act
the way I'd like to become...and voila! It's a fact!
Of course, I can change the script...and I ought...
when I feel too important...Life's profound enough...
so I can't take myself too seriously...Learn to love...
and for that script, I used others so I may be taught...

In my play, 'to control' is dominant, is prevalent...I know...
Yet, nearly everything I've asked for has been a go...
I thought I had forgiven my past...but, not quite...
Taking a tour of elapsed time...revisiting my memory,
I sensed...I perceived bits and pieces of my past story...
a little anger, some mistrust, even, still a bit uptight...
It's time to let it go...to clear my spirit of this plight...

It's taken a long time...not overnight...but years...
to reach a sort of a balance...to overcome my fears...
or at least some of them...Life was not meant to heed
when I could justify...Becoming accountable was tough...
Compliance, candour, tolerance, was some of the stuff
I needed to endorse... if I truly wanted to succeed...

When I do what I do, I usually get what I get...
not something different...What more can I expect?
Therefore I've really been trying to do my best...
Do I always succeed? No! But, the success rate
has improved...and that's something to celebrate...
For the most part I've passed my different tests...

I was feeling comfortable in my life-style...yet...
something was missing...what? Unsure...so I let
God bring in new ideas, new people...His decision...
I've come to understand He knows what's best for me...
so, I accept that He's trying to make me happy...
I've now met someone who gives me much aspiration...

I recall asking God for a friend...someone to talk to...
yet, I wanted more than that...So I added more clues...
which included to share my thoughts, my beliefs,
my values, my feelings...He presented you to me...
What a gift!! Your openness...your sincerity....
your honesty...What more could I ask...What a relief!

I'm not sure why God sent you to me...but I do...
Because I asked...and He felt I needed the likes of you...
Being by your side...laughing, talking, sharing...is so nice...
Into my life...you've put back much joy and pleasure ...
and...I've shown you a different approach...that's for sure...
If this continues as such...One day at a time will then suffice...

One Of Life's Greatest Gift...Choices...

I've always wanted to write a poem on Henry Ward Beecher's inspiring prose "Life," for whenever I read this passage...and I have read it often...I have often asked myself the same question he asks, 'how will I accept life...' I decided to pursue this question, by accepting the different choices each situation offers...and, often, virtually by trail and error, I have formulated...I have devised a style that suits me.

If it wasn't for choices...the different options, the choice of alternatives...the array, the assortment of choices, and the abundance and the range of choices...I'm not sure what life would consist of...I live every day by making a multitude of choices...from the mundane to very important. That is how I've become the person that I am...through life experiences, through choices...and in life there is always change...therefore more choices...so I can continue to better me...

If this isn't life's greatest gift, it's certainly close...

One Of Life's Greatest Gift... Choices...

God asks no man whether he will accept life.
That is not the choice.
You must take it.
The only choice is how.

Henry Ward Beecher

As I look at my only choice..."How to accept life"...
I need to be taught, so I may learn to develop, to derive...
What are the lessons I must learn so I may strive
to attain a gratifying life? Many teachers will contrive
obstacles...hurdles...so that I'm capable to survive...
that I may experience life's treasures...and not be deprived...

What are the lessons the teachers are teaching? Much...
To understand who I am, I often need to be nudged...
To survive I need friends...examples by whom I will judge
my own actions...An intimate partner, with whom I'll trudge
many paths...who will be both an inspiration and a crutch...
Someone I can share my soul with and also share a touch...

Only by looking backwards can I connect the dots...
not by looking forward...Another lesson that was taught...
and there are many... Life is a maze where much is brought...
to untangle this labyrinth of energy, without getting caught
in the cracks, corners and web...Many sessions are sought...
Each dot connected reflects my model of 'what I ought'...

And, 'the ought' what are they? What need I achieve?
Well, they're moral obligations...something I need to weave...
creating a design...an outline...so I may come to believe
that my intentions are honourable...not like a thief...
To get past 'the wants,' there is much I need to leave...
The first to go is ego...Then much good can I retrieve...
Tell me...what good will I get back if I follow this plan?

I am promised choices...not stuff written in the sand...
false promises...blown away with a touch of élan...
of flamboyance...pretending everything is so grand...
I was taught to be forth-right...able to take a stand...
With empathy and trust...I walk hand in hand...

In God's plan...Where do I fit in...What is my role?
I ask: "What is role? How do I decide on my goals?"
Sharing of myself is a responsibility I can unfold...
I can be trustworthy, dependable...or a real A-hole...
Again choices...I can give opinions...pretending to know...
or, I can be humble...by following my conscience...my soul...

In asking 'How', God gives me choices...and the freedom
to pursue...and, to make mistakes...The lessons learnt come
from listening, from exploring...firing-up the passion...
I guess that's God's way to show me right from wrong...
If I use honesty, open-mindedness and willingness...seldom
will I error...Could this truly be the price of admission...
admission that I'm flawed...and that's okay...for us humans...

Life's a very good teacher...It teaches much is contrary...
that God's plan is not a dilemma...merely a mystery...
which comprises mystique, and a bit of obscurity...
It explains to me that life is an expedition ...a journey...
that is only traveled one day at a time...and, not to worry...
At journey's end...life will still be full of ambiguity...

Life really does offer many gifts in different designs...
wrapped uniquely with special feelings and signs.
A nice thing...most of these options have no time-line...
plus, the choices I make, for the most part, are mine...

I Will Always Continue Loving You...

Life is not eternal...at least not our physical life. This poem touches somewhat on that aspect. The setting is in a Nursing Home, yet the last verse happens in a hospital.

Looking over this poem...if I had wanted to make it look like it was a young child being portrayed...all I would have had to do was re-write the last verse. The similarities, quite often, are so close...The parent taking care of the child...The child taking care of the parent...

As a parent, I don't always like or agree with my children's choices... but one thing I can say is I have always loved them...and I suspect I will always continue loving them...

I Will Always Continue Loving You...

Why am I in trouble again? I don't understand...
They always seem to be displeased...and they demand
that I listen...They use such big words...How can I
know what they want, even though I really try...
yet, It's not my fault...I sometime wander off...
I guess they want my attention...I hear that cough...
      Here we go again...I really don't stand a chance...
      They sure do lack tolerance and patience...

I remember my dad telling me quite a while back:
"Don't talk...Just listen...That's how you learn the knack..."
Well, today, I want to explain how I feel to them...
how this man questioned me, then wrote with his pen...
I'm tired of listening...Why do they always say to me:
"We've heard that a 100 times before...just let it be..."
      I love it so much when they stroke my tired skin
      It feels so nice...so loving...making me grin...

My reading capabilities are so very derisory...
yet, I love it when someone reads me a story.
I go for the scary ones...but, I know I shouldn't...
Sometimes I'm the character they're trying to hunt...
and I awake screaming...It usually takes a while
to get my bearing...realizing it aien't me on trial...
      But, so it seems, they don't read too often anymore...
      It appears everyone's always grumpy and sore...

Some of that garbage they call food makes me sick...
When they aien't looking...chucking it out is the trick...
Sometimes they get so mad when they finally realize
what I did...Explaining is useless...so I tell white lies...
At times...I sense...they'd love to give me a spanking...
I'm glad they don't follow through with their hankering...
      Once in a while I'd love having potato chips...
      I prefer it with dill or garlic...my two favourite dips...

Not that long ago I tried to run away and hide…
Boy, when they found me, I learnt the word 'to comply'…
They made sure I understood what was their regulations.
So what if they feel annoyed…I too have frustrations…
My space to meander is so limited…I could scream…
Every now and then, I too need to let off steam…
        Often I imagine myself alone on some trail…
        no worries…at peace…leaving behind all the details…

What's embarrassing are the times I still wet the bed…
Those times…when that happens…I really dread…
Unfortunately, I have no real sense of detection…
Now, they've put on a rubber sheet for protection…
If it occurs too often, they force me to wear a diaper…
Humiliation can't describe my feelings of despair…
        The words and tone my loved one's use to scold me
        really hurt…What's the big issue…it's only pee…

I don't understand what they mean, when they suggest
I change my attitude …Not sure if this is merely a jest…
Many of the things they perceive as not being so good
really irritate me…For example: My t-shirt with a hood…
or, my pants I've worn forever…They're so comfortable..
This new attitude…Am I merely to comply…to enable?
        I wish some of my old friends would come and visit…
        But, they don't…No wonder I feel like I'm in the pits…

I thought The Home was bad…This stinking hospital is worse…
Everyone is walking on egg shells…They're all so terse…
I love my children very much, and I know they're trying
their best to make me comfortable…But, why all the crying?
I realize since the stroke…I can't speak, and I love to nap…
I guess, to them, that means I've now become quite a handicap…
They're always speaking in a hush…in low, soft voices…
        yet, I hear and understand all…including all of their choices…
        It seems my life is coming to a close…Nothing they can do…

I have no regrets…All that I ask…and this isn't new…
With God's consent, I will always continue loving you too…

Just For Today...

This is a very special day for us...We are so happy you are a part of this occasion, this festivities. We could have gone and gotten married in some exotic place, which is fine...or we could have had a huge ceremony... but we decided on a more intimate setting, presided by our friend Debbie, and then a few weeks later, we gathered with our family and a few friends to truly celebrate our wedding.

My family loves to party...any little excuse we use to get together and party...Because of this, we have become great organizers...

Kathy and I are so happy you could be a big part of this day...our day...I love Kathy very much, and I want to continue this...and I can if I remember that I can love her for this day...just for today...If I keep this in mind, then our love will only enhance and grow.

Just For Today...

The story of the fisherman...casting his line into the water...
hauling in much good...yet, some flawed...is very similar
to how we want our story to be...Together, we will cast
our line...ours lives...hopefully having dealt with our past...
and. keeping in mind, no matter what, all will work-out fine...
just as long as we're willing to live one day at a time...

We already know our past...and we know we can't return...
but, we can and should use this knowledge that we may learn...
And, our future...well, who knows? So, today is all we control...
With the guidance of the greatest Fisherman of all...we will troll
for intimacy, for truth, for love...the things we need to catch...
so that these feelings...into our hearts and minds will be etched...

Looking back...we both have much to be thankful for...
Family...friends...health...plus, now we have each other...
Is this enough? Today we say yes! For that's all we have
is today...therefore we need to share, to care and to laugh...
Just for today, we need to be in contact with our Creator...
asking for advice and support...We want to concur, not deter...

We are two individuals...through marriage, joined as one...
We've both experienced sadness and sorrow...and then some...
In understanding grief, we are now able to appreciate joy...
We love each others company...We are past the stage of coy...
In asking our Higher Power to lead us...to show us the way...
we are learning to live life on life's terms...Just For Today...

113

A Chat With God.

Written by Al Hagman.

After our small intimate wedding, we took a two week break...then had a celebration with more family and friends. At this celebration, my brother Richard was our presenter. He had asked Al to write a few verses for this occasion. Al was so enthused with this task...he wrote two poems. The poem titled *Someone To Love* is very quaint...and Kathy and I thank him for it...It's a poem we will cherish.

My sister Gisele read both poems at our ceremony...The poem we chose was *A Chat With God*. A very touching, thoughtful, considerate poem ...quite solicitous...

Thank-you Al!

A Chat With God.

Two lives, living in different worlds
Unknown to one another, parallel
Growing up in innocence
Until the innocence is shattered
Each of their mothers, guiding lights taken
Oh God, too early

Still life goes on, and each find love
Not with each other, not yet
But for a time there is peace
Until the peace is broken
Hearts turn sour, shattered loves
My God, it hurts

The test continues, pain and suffering
Life lashing wildly on weary backs
Knees buckle from crosses too heavy
No one to listen, no one to soothe
Lowered heads leaning against the storm
Dear God, please help

So then only time, time needed to heal
To crumble the walls of protection
And soften the hardened hearts
Afraid to love again, to feel again
Destined to be alone, new love will never be
Why God, why not?

And then without a sign, against all probability
Their hearts are joined, their souls enwrapped
The dark clouds are pierced by the sunshine
A smile sprouts where none would grow
And loneliness is smashed against the rocks
Dear God, could it really be?

Since then is an altered state, a schism
No longer is there a single impression on the pillow
No longer will a road traveled alone
Someone to talk to, to grow old with
To laugh with, to cry with, to love
And God, Thank You

Playing The Hand I've Been Dealt.

I always liked this title...although it's taken many years to finally put a poem to it. The reason being...I'm still writing my story, I'm still playing in the game, and in my particular hand, I'm still the dealer. Maybe I'm too early for this poem...perhaps, as time goes on, I will make additions to this poem, for life does continue...Time will tell.

I wrote this poem based on comparisons, based on choices...because for me that's life. I always have to choose what I feel is the correct way for me in each particular situation. As an example, as a child/ young adult, my parents were in control, but on my own, I evaluated their choices and decided what I felt was right and wrong...and finally realized they were only human, and had done the best they could...When it came my turn to raise my kids, I know I made many mistakes, and I know my children will be/are re-evaluating my teachings, and hopefully they'll understand that I too am human. I could give examples of bad marriage, good marriage, bad friend. good friends... and the list goes on...all experiences of my life...and yes, I made the final verdict for myself on each decision. But I could only do that after analyzing all the evidence. When dealing with people, they have a big play in my final decision...Ex: Divorce.

As my life continues, I've learnt many things, felt many emotions... One of the things that I'm finally starting to learn is that forgiveness is the answer to everything...everything. Life being the fine teacher that it is, I'm still being taught how to go about doing this through the shuffling and dealing of the cards in my game of life...and no doubt will continue for the rest of my time...

Playing The Hand I've Been Dealt.

Life can be compared to a river…so mysterious…
At times quite calm, yet invites the curious…
Other times deep and brooding…quite serious…
Depending on conditions, it may become furious…

My life is full of many opposing feelings…
My teachers called this revealing and concealing…
Of the lessons I learnt, most I could well relate…
yet, there are some I really have to contemplate…
I have to see and comprehend to appreciate…

To truly understand my hand,
comparisons are in my command…
I need to be aware of the disparity…
the differences…to appreciate parity…
How else will I come to understand?

My childhood was, or so it seems, similar
to most kids growing up…ruled by adults…
Looking back, time really did go by in a blur,
yet, in that moment it felt slow, and the fault
lay at the feet of my parents…their control…
Finally…I realized my betterment was the goal…
yet, because of my distrust, it took it's toll…

Going down this river with its many twist and turns…
the current is running strong…not easy to discern…
The banks are fairly narrow…much to be concerned…
In life, this is a time to be aware…a time to learn…

118

When choosing between the options of choices or indifference...
indifference won hands down...It was easier not to choose...
My attitude was "who cares"...To me that made sense...
especially when my best friend and confidant, Sir Booze
was around...I felt people owed me...Why? I'm unsure...
and that's honest...My drinking...that was a big factor...
Because of it jealousy, anger and resentments did occur...

Responsibilities were thrust upon me by default...
Because of my outlook and decisions, I was accountable
for my actions...yet, I denied...others were at fault...
In my eyes, I did not want to be responsible...
To blame was easy...therefore I used that course
as my justification...I finally had to admit recourse...
My obligations were mine...something I had to endorse...

The banks have widened... The river is much deeper...
The under-current seems so calm...a real sleeper...
Oh, but be very careful...it feels like the Grim Reaper...
Sounds of water ahead...The ride will be much steeper...

During this period I had conflict in truth-lies ...
which caused much variance with my emotions..
I was young and wanted to believe, yet my eyes
felt like a chemist, mixing different potions
of trust-deceit...It didn't feel nor smell right...
Putting the test tube truth/suspicions to the light,
shaking it, weighing it...I trusted my psyche...

Also, during this time the struggle of love-hate
came into play. An emotion that's never-ending...
This passion weighed heavy on my plate...
What a draining feeling...defending or mending...
To love...to adore, to cherish, to feel affection for...

119

feelings right from the nucleus...right from the core...
How can this beauty die? How can this be no more?
Hate...this avid emotion has many facets...
Spouse, parents, friends, employers are just a few...
It matters not how, why or who caused it...
No...the pot of repulsiveness is a foul stew...
Having experienced this...I wish it on no one...
Trying to, yet unable to endure, is just no fun...
I left the table starving...after all was said and done...

I traveled these rough waters for quite sometime,
always looking for indications of sort...a sign...
something...to help me get through these trying times...
Finally, a break...Through the clouds I could feel sun shine...

My ego...my self-image...was being taken to the cleaners...
A hard lesson...showing me that I was not so important...
Talk about deflation for someone who was such a dreamer...
I struggled mightily...I was not ready to be compliant...
I finally let go of my narcissism during this rocky ride...
Humility made me see clearly exactly what pride
was trying to attain...my downfall, my demise...It always lied...

Life was changing, but the clashes were always there...
Anger was my close friend, yet a much closer enemy...
Always present or just barely behind the scene...where
in a moments notice either I contain or set it free...
As a foe, my anger was very vindictive, very hurtful...
As an ally, it taught me awareness and what was my roll...
bringing me calmness, and a chance to consult with my soul...

I was slowly starting to realize my wrongs...
Yet, resentment lingered on...so did my friend ire...
I truly loved the past...comparable to a favorite song...
You know the one...the roamer, the cheater, the liar...
It gave me comfort...an invisible security blanket...

After many encores, I came to understand my many regrets...
Fault became forgiveness...I could start repaying my debts...
The current was still quite choppy, thought at a glance,
the waters looked a lot smoother in the distance...
The vessel moved with the waves, creating a flowing dance...
My body was sore, so I pulled to shore to rest, to relax...

During my growing up period, I had to encounter
many lessons...One...my anger was based on fear...
I felt this was just a part of my makeup...for sure...
and, subconsciously, I wanted nothing to do with mirrors...
To combat this feeling, I had to become the student...
I truly had to listen to the many teachers that were sent...
They taught me that faith in a Higher Power paid the rent...

I was also taught that although life did not stand still,
I didn't always have to be in a hurry to go nowhere...
Many lessons in serenity were practiced and instilled...
How? By experiencing the steps of my personal stairs...
In spite of everything...today is still full of stress,
yet, I attained closure to much unfinished business...
I learnt forgiveness is the key to this whole process...

Did I truly choose my fate, my own providence?
I can't see where I have garnered enough credence
to justify this thought...The hand I was dealt
certainly wasn't all my choosing...that's what I felt...
Yet, of these cards, I do receive much emotional wealth...

A closer look at this question portrays me as the one
who is the dealer...I have influence on what's being done...
I have a right to choose...Of all the issues thrown my way...
for the most part, I have the privilege of the final say...
with the help of my Higher Power...and for that I pray...

Not that far ahead, the water looked cool and clear...
The rest felt good...On the banks I noticed a deer...
Looking ahead, I could see a hazy outline of pier...
A feeling of relief...I was happy the end was so near.

121

In The Eyes Of The Beholder.

I went to Vietnam for a wedding...My nephew, Jason, married Thuy, a beautiful Vietnamese woman. What an experience. I went with the intentions of meeting the locals, experiencing their food and culture. I did all of that, and more. I loved the whole trip...I felt so comfortable. Thuy's family was exceptional hosts...and such nice, kind, friendly people. These people are peasants...They have a small plot of land, shared by many, to grow rice, plus they have a few coconut trees. They also have a few pigs, cows, chickens, yet, in spite of this, I still feel they and poverty are very close neighbors...They really know no other life-style, yet, no matter what life throws at them, you can feel their love for each other.

We were fortunate to visit some of Vietnam. Such a lovely country, but poor. We heard lots of sad stories, witnessed some real poverty. Vietnam, I would classify as a very poor country controlled by a Communist Government. That's where this poem stems from...my observations.

I decided to write this poem on comparisons. That turned out to be tougher than I had anticipated. Why? Because of that choice, I never wrote about The Vietnamese, per se, but I wrote more about the feelings of the capitalist culture/people versus the oppressed, dictator culture/people. These feelings came from my experiences in Vietnam.

The capitalist is so lucky, through the eyes of the peasant, for they have so much material wealth...where the peasant, on the other hand, understands that life will probably continue as such for him...but he would sure love to try some of "the good life" for a while...If I was in his shoes, without a doubt I would too.

It certainly would be nice to find a harmonizing balance.

This poem is dedicated to Thien & Thi Phan...May God bless!

122

In The Eyes Of The Beholder.

To evaluate two totally different cultures,
and, at the same time, try and be objective...
a lot of variance my mind does deliver.
These differences have too many whiffs,
too many traces. I can't help but not compare...
so, it becomes a balancing act of what to share,
what to keep, what's priority... and to be aware
that those whom recognize and accept truth are rare...

I could never survive in your environment...never...
What with all the people barely making ends meet,
and it doesn't matter how hard you try to endeavor,
to gain ground...Life is always a continuous feat.
Poverty kills many...and often...with no qualms...
That's not for me...I want little stress...lots of calm.

Usually your government is very autocratic...
habitually oppressive...therefore family is vital...
Cohesion is the key...all must follow the same stride.
You get to know what's important...real quick...
dependence on each other...being responsible...
resulting in a discipline which all must abide.

My children are raised on instant gratification.
This type of love has no joy...it's meaningless...
then I wonder why they have so little appreciation.
A real quandary...All it seems to do is create a mess.
Like a baby lamb, I follow the example of my peers...
yet, when things go wrong, they simply disappear.

Kids nurtured strictly on material pleasures,
become bored and disenchanted ...no spirit...
Many choose weird alternatives for their cravings...
But, on the other hand, you have a real treasure...
Even though all must work with tenacity and grit.
This treasure: A feeling of self-respect, of belonging.

How can I pass on my foundation, my morals,
if the lifestyle I lead is to lie and cheat?
I can't! A snake's life is to slink and crawl...
so, if that's me, I'll convey this to all I meet.
My standards don't hold a whole lot of water...
and my boat is sinking...without a care or bother.

To become someone that doesn't become you,
thinking you're better than the person you were...
is so wrong...You become the loser in a fools game.
You feel "wealth" is all material. That's not true...
Emotions, feelings, love...should be a greater lure,
but they aren't...With pleasure there's always pain.

"In God's eyes we are all equal." says the old adage.
Yet, our culture feels so sophisticated, so couth...
How can we be equal? How can we be on the same page?
By the mind seeing what the heart wishes weren't truths...
If poverty is a killer...well, so is prosperity...
It kills emotions and the spirit with alacrity.

When looking through the mind's eye...life isn't fair...
To invent some sanity...dreams are the sole way.
You can't make a new start, but you can a new ending.
Successes may be few...in fact they may even be rare...
but count them...and say thanks at the end of the day...
Failures...that's life...Fences always need mending.

Possibly by having less is better than having more...
That's a real contradiction for a capitalist...
but there may be truth to this teaching, this lore.
Our viewpoint is sick...indicated by the big cyst...
full of avarice and insatiability...full of pus.
Forget not...He is not a choice...He is a must.

I see in your eyes that you'd be willing to give-up
almost anything for this perceived good life...
and, who could blame you...Imagination
relays abundance in all material things.
What's needed is a balance...so all can access
education, health, food, shelter, warmth...
A real soothing for the mind, body and soul...

Tell me truths, tell me stories ...I am The Beholder...
Be not afraid...If you need...please use my shoulder.
I'm not there to give of my values, my beliefs...
but to respect and observe your joys and grief's.
I want to see, hear, smell, feel, and touch...
I really desire to experience my position as such.

Emotions Guided By Fear...

I decided to do an inventory about some important issues that affect me and my sons in our relationship. What this made me discover...which I knew all along...was I employed control as a means to attain my wants. Anger was my excellent conduit to fear. Somehow, and I'm not sure when, this process backfired on me. I rarely attained the goals I was seeking...as hard as I tried...Many times I lost control, and my mind, my emotions would revert to fear. We were not a well family...thanks to me...

To make changes, today is as good a day as any. I can't predict change on behalf of my boys, they are responsible for that, but I certainly can make changes to better me...to better our relationship...and a good start is by using love not fear as my catalyst...Only then I might have a chance...

Emotions Guided By Fear...

Everything negative is guided by fear...
Why is that? And, it's always so near,
like an active volcano spewing steam
and hot molten ash...destroying my dreams.
With fear comes a big loss of control...
and anger is the tool used when I troll.
Often I get caught up in the current,
floundering about and full of resentment...
Before time elapses I am totally helpless,
wondering "How did I get into this mess?"
Often, destructive physical thoughts appear.
Everything negative is guided by fear...
Why is that?...

My emotions ask: "What about respect?"

Good question...Do I consider respect as lack?
If so, do I feel that I give the respect back?
Well, quite often I've been a bit slack
in saying thanks, yet very quick to criticize.
I get lost in the trivial, wanting to justify
my thought process by suggesting that my eyes
see things that may not always be completely clear,
yet, contradict by letting my mouth get in gear...
or, suggest there are many things I hear,
supposedly truth, but which are innuendos.
In these I'm quick to fault, by hitting below
the belt. This causes much anguish, many woes.

Answer: Respect is quite deficient on my part,
           and needs a tune-up before I can start
             to change. What I need is a heart to heart,
             a newness of attitude, to help me depart.

My emotions now ask: "What about control/ arguments?"

Tough question. What do I feel control means?
With certain issues I like to battle the stream,
therefore, I like to see things done as I deem.
Now, if this was a fight of right or wrong.
good or bad, win or lose, shunned or belong,
then, the decision made I would not prolong.
But, the control in question is about power...
to humiliate, waiting to see them cower,
while thinking I'm so great, the majestic tower.
Why do I play this game...and the whimsy rules?
Is it low self-esteem causing me to be cruel?
Or, perhaps fear, making me act like a fool?

The question also asked about arguments...
How do they get started? Who gives consent?
If so, there must be feelings of contempt?
In certain situations, my personage is commanding,
wanting my way and mad if my understanding
is questioned. I have a right to be demanding...
especially if I want to leave an impression.
To do that I need to get into a real session
of yelling...just to teach them a good lesson.
Of course, this type of fight no one's the winner.
The pot keeps boiling...there's lots to stir...
then another volatile eruption occurs.

Answer: Control and argue...two big, big issues...
         things I learnt from peers as being true.
         Today, I know these are wrong, and I must pursue
         new direction...yet, I find it so hard to do.

128

I'm thinking: "What about bitterness that leads to anger?"

People want to do things their own way,
and who can blame them? Really, I can't say
what's right or wrong…unless I'm the prey…
then I become defensive and aggressive.
If it affects my codes, I become provocative.
and during these times I'm not too cognitive…
When this occurs, more often than not,
I forget a lot of the things I was taught…
Sometimes I feel like a misanthrope.
My mind's centered on one thing…to defend.
If I don't calm down, I lose my focus, then
my cynicism starts…the beginning of the end.

Answer: Often I feel like I'm in some forest
completely lost. I need to sit down…to rest…
to think it through…figure out what's best,
to act not react, engaging in my souls caress.

My mind asks: "What are my feelings towards youth?"

When I was a drinking man, I thought everyone
drank like me. Little did I know only some
did…Most drank sociably and had fun.
With the youth of today, perhaps the same sort
of thing is happening again…I live in my port…
judging all seas as rough without any report.
How do I assume this? Around me is turbulence,
so, there must be commotion everywhere, hence
my version must be correct of what I sense…
therefore I need to protect myself from harm.
When the seas become calm, I sound the alarm.
How can my report be so wrong? I'll be darn!

129

Yet, having said what I've said, today's youth
seem to be more demanding and quite uncouth...
or am I judging again? I'm searching for truth.
I know in my case, there's a lot of disrespect...
and that hurts. One thing, I can certainly detect
is their lying...their stealing...things I won't forget...
They seem to display defiance to authority figures,
not just me. Their friends do the same, that's for sure...
Drugs...soft and hard...are so prevalent, as is liquor.
The wisdom statement: 'How you treat your parents
will slap you in the face many times hence...'
Their turn will come as it did me. Makes sense?

Answer: I feel handicapped...a man in a sling...
          I'm so damn caught-up in my own thing.
          Because I haven't learnt how to give wings,
          I suffer the results of what control brings.

A big question asked: "Why is money always a problem?"

This is a major problem in our disputes,
and causes much anger on my part, to boot.
Whenever discussed, the results are always moot.
I could get into the rhetoric of my own business,
where, often, looks are deceiving, and the stress...
When I mention this, they laugh as in jest...
"The store pays for lots...what about your money?
You owe me!" What I owe are: When you have a runny
nose, I care for your health. When your tummy
starts grumbling, I buy you food. I owe you shelter,
clothes on your back, and education...so you may confer.
Those are the material things I owe you...for sure,

What do I owe you emotionally? Love, security,
guidance…helping you make The Step into reality.
I know I've not done a great job, actually.
Through all of this, the issue is some of the above,
but very little…No, what you feel aren't enough…
are privileges. True! That's where I use tough love.
For example, when a job's well done…I compensate,
yet, you'll do the opposite and think you still rate…
then become defiant when I refuse to cooperate.
I withhold monetary allowance so you may learn
some responsibilities, which are of your concern.
Don't bite the hand feeding you, or you'll get burned.

Answer: This dilemma, this predicament requires
            those whom have learnt how to conspire…
        I don't see a resolution to this quagmire…
        though…it could work if all players had a desire.

I need to know: "Where does the Higher Power fit in?"

Through all of this I am smart enough to know,
eventhough I can put on a pretty good show,
I have little power or control of the flow…
Unfortunately, I still try play God at times,
attaining no success, inspite of being his mime.
It's getting better. I'm learning to read the signs…
understand the reasons, by talking to my heart,
digging into my feelings…pulling out the dart
from my wounded esteems…seeking to part
these different emotions, so I may learn
to use them properly. That's when I must turn
to my Higher Power, and give Him my concerns.
Now, the issues presented…what needs to be done?
Harness control and anger. They are poison…
Loosen up, ask for guidance…Enjoy…Have fun…

"What have I learnt through this study?"

I felt the answers before starting this process,
but I didn't know the solutions…only guesses.
Contradictions? Lots shifting through this mess.
When I brought out my feelings, opening the door
to my emotions, I realized what was in store…
Two passions, two paragons I strive for
are truth and honesty…giving me integrity,
a lot of moral strength…not acrimony,
that pill of resentment…I need stability…
I'll take my responsibility for the harm I've borne,
for that is only right…yet, I won't conform
to the wrongs of others. I know…when I scorn
people for their lack of desire in owning up to
their misdeeds…it is wrong…It has nothing to do
with me, I can't change them…and that is the clue…
I can forgive, and only change me to guarantee no rue…

I love them very much…The lessons they've taught me…
if I'm really honest…has been nothing's for free…
except my love for them…Mistakes have made me see
that my intentions were right…my approach was wrong…
Because of my actions, my amends I need not prolong…
As a family, unity is the key…each one of us belongs…

English Class Poetry.

The following three poems were written while taking English 101. I needed this class to obtain my Social Worker Diploma, and part of this English program called for poetry writing. My professor, Sandra, was a great inspiration for me...She taught me much in this English Class.

Enjoy!

Two Unlit Candles.

Sandra, our English 101 teacher wanted us to use our imagination and to write creatively.

Why I wrote this particular poem, I'm unsure. Sandra wanted three different types of poems...1) erotic, yet subliminal...and, of course, imagination. 2) Pensive, yet unusual...and imagination. 3) Fantasy, yet persuasive and imagination.

Two Unlit Candles is the first one I wrote. Sandra's comments on this one were: "Imagination, subtle, sexy! Very good". The people involved was a figment of my imagination... unfortunately.

Two Unlit Candles.

Your body, my body like two unlit candles,
long, slender cylinders of molten wax
facing one another in our holder,
our bed. The twisted fibres used, yet never used.

I love watching your body quiver
from anticipation of the vibes
my burning fingertips will send you.
Caressing your breast, the candle's wick is lit.

Your torso shudders as I gently touch.
Our kisses penetrate deeper and deeper
as my entry is smooth and waxen. Our motion,
the candle light, flickers so, so tenderly.

Our movement becomes stronger and faster
as the wax drips from our candle-like bodies.
Our surrounding air, now in a wave pattern,
predicts turbulence. The halo light flickers wildly.

We're out of control, we've lost it completely.
Our love juices descending down on to the holder.
The flame, ever so slowly, fades away,
leaving your body, my body like two unlit candles.

135

Contemplation.

This is the second poem written...the one on "Pensive, yet unusual... and of course imagination."

I wrote this in about 15 minutes. Actually, it was fun to write. It's exactly what Sandra had asked for, even though it's a no-brainer.

Sandra's comments: " What can I say?" That says for me as well.

Contemplation.

Sitting here contemplating,
wondering
unsure of whatever happened
to your dream,
my dream,
our fantasy of pure physical and emotional love.
Where are you?
You meant so much to me,
as I to you,
and we to us, us, us.
Oh! I miss you.   PLOP!

Clouds.

This is the third poem written...the one on "Fantasy, yet persuasive... and of course imagination."

Clouds was so much fun to write, for I am often in the clouds... wondering, imagining, thinking, feeling. It's funny, but all games are won, all questions answered, all problems resolved, all turmoil is settled...when the mind is romping through the clouds.

Sandra's comments: " I love this! Very Nice. Keep this one forever, and put it on your fridge for your kids...Great!" It felt wonderful reading such a comment...Thanks Sandra.

Clouds.

I love it up here in paradise.
God, what an elated, sumptuous feeling...
Jumping...Rolling...Flipping...Floating...
above and over, beyond and yond
on my suspended, billowy softness.
No! This can't be Dante's cloud nine
for I have nothing to prove
nothing to be exalted about,
yet, here I am in my spiritual heaven...
so very free, so very warm, so very happy.
Wow! I love it up here in my paradise...

At The End Of The Day...Does It Really Matter?

Good question! Lately I've been looking back into my past to see how far I've come...and in all actuality, I've travelled quite a ways forward...but, really, is that so important? I feel it is. Back in the "good old days," I can surely recall many days of quilt, of fear, of remorse, of anger...especially at me, but always trying to masquerade it by blaming others...I couldn't accept that perhaps it was my fault...yet, deep-down, I knew it was. Those were suppose to have been "real good times". A lot were good times, but more were not. What it ended up being was a good learning period...I made a whole lot of mistakes back then...and got burnt often enough. Thank God I remember some of them...

Would I like to go back to those times? No! Therefore I've taken on a new type of life-style, which gives me a lot more contentment, more self-esteem, more reasons to want to get up in the morning. I've gained a conscious, I've taken on responsibilities...I've become more accountable. Why would I do that if at the end of the day it means sweet tweet?

If, at the end of the day there is no Higher Power, well I can say I had a good life, I helped others, I tried to make my surroundings a better place and I feel good about that...BUT...if there is a Higher Power at the end of the line...maybe He will forgive, even though I abused of my privileges...but I do feel that by following my conscience and try and do what's right for me, I'm a happier person...and, who knows!!! Maybe it doesn't matter.

At The End Of The day...Does It Really Matter?

How can I have a real future without having dealt
with my past? I can't! If I try to be sneaky...stealth...
I hurt no one but me. Today, I share my past wealth...
so others can learn from my mistakes...my blunders...
I need to feel happiness after having felt anger...
joy/sadness...serenity/pain...Today, I'm often in wonder...
often in awe...at how my life is changing...has changed...
My life, actually, is something of an honour, a privilege...
thanks to my God, whose given me freedom to change...

Going a bit deeper into my past...digging up stuff...
I seemed to always want to give the impact I was tough...
but I wasn't... It wasn't hard to figure out my bluff.
I was so negative... looking at how I couldn't do something
instead of how I could...An attitude worth zilch...nothing...
My future was mirrored in my past...Ouch...What a sting...
I was searching for outward happiness ...the cause of my plight...
With much help, I finally gave up living only for the night...
Today, I search within...to attain an awareness...an insight...

In all my wisdom...It took me many years to realize
I had choices...In all things I could be foolish or wise...
follow my conscience or my ego...tell truth or tell lies...
It was God's choices, the people whom entered my life...
My choice was to keep those who caused less strife...
and the rest...I let walk away...This helped me survive...
God's job is to keep sending...My job is to screen...
On some of those I let go, I should have been more keen...
but...I can't afford to think of what might have been...

I like my privacy, yet I still enjoy my friends...
and the ones I have, really seem to comprehend,
and accept my quirky ways...I rarely have to defend
my actions. I've come to know and understand stability...
My friends taught me openness and susceptibility...
because I've shared some of my vulnerabilities...
Often they would suggest a different point of view,
another way to approach...offering something new...
Of course, the final choice was mine, for I paid the dues...

Life's a funny thing...I actually didn't change a lot
over time...in spite of all the lessons I've been taught...
I may have thought I had...but honestly...I've really not...
Yet...the different paths I encounter in my lifetime...
well, those certainly did...Sometimes I've had to climb...
other times it was bumpy, and still others, the path was fine.
It wasn't because I chose happiness or to feel blue...
or because I always liked to stir the pot of stew...
No...I got to where I got because I was suppose to...

In trying to learn to become somewhat mellow...
and, let me tell you, for me, that process is slow...
I must give away this knowledge so that I may grow...
I've learnt that success and failure are never final...
and neither count very much...no matter the style...
Do the best you can until you reach your final mile...
Life's like a bank account...assets balance out the debt...
Happiness is the interest gathered...and it's a sure bet.
The more we give of self, the more assets we will get...

Ah! The devil's advocate in me desires to cause debate...

God forgives...regardless, according to philosophers,
if one asks for exoneration...Therefore, anything can occur...
So I ask...At the end of the day...does it really matter?

LaVergne, TN USA
13 November 2010
204700LV00004B/2/P